Early Praise for *Rust Brain Teasers*

This is a wonderful collection of brain teasers that will not only introduce you to the most peculiar Rust quirks concepts but can also teach you a few interesting things about programming as well. Whether you want to use Rust as your primary language or not (well, you definitely should), this book has something great to offer for everyone.

➤ **Vladyslav Batyrenko**
Software Engineer

Herbert's latest book explores some of Rust's oddities that are sure to catch you out a few times as a beginner. Each puzzle is short and clear, the explanations are great and full of knowledge and wisdom. Highly recommend picking up this book for an afternoon full of head-scratching Rust programming puzzles, and I guarantee you won't be able to put this down.

➤ **Olivia Ifrim**

Rust Brain Teasers

Exercise Your Mind

Herbert Wolverson

The Pragmatic Bookshelf

Raleigh, North Carolina

Many of the designations used by manufacturers and sellers to distinguish their products are claimed as trademarks. Where those designations appear in this book, and The Pragmatic Programmers, LLC was aware of a trademark claim, the designations have been printed in initial capital letters or in all capitals. The Pragmatic Starter Kit, The Pragmatic Programmer, Pragmatic Programming, Pragmatic Bookshelf, PragProg and the linking *g* device are trademarks of The Pragmatic Programmers, LLC.

Every precaution was taken in the preparation of this book. However, the publisher assumes no responsibility for errors or omissions, or for damages that may result from the use of information (including program listings) contained herein.

For our complete catalog of hands-on, practical, and Pragmatic content for software developers, please visit *https://pragprog.com*.

The team that produced this book includes:

CEO: Dave Rankin
COO: Janet Furlow
Managing Editor: Tammy Coron
Development Editor: Tammy Coron
Copy Editor: L. Sakhi MacMillan
Indexing: Potomac Indexing, LLC
Layout: Gilson Graphics
Founders: Andy Hunt and Dave Thomas

For sales, volume licensing, and support, please contact *support@pragprog.com*.

For international rights, please contact *rights@pragprog.com*.

ISBN-13: 978-1-680509-17-5
Book version: P1.0—March 2022

*To Henry, my loyal canine coding companion
of thirteen years—who sadly didn't live to see
the book's release.*

Contents

Acknowledgments

This book would not have been possible without the patience, support, and love of my wife, Mel Wolverson.

Margaret Eldridge deserves special thanks for suggesting that I write this book. I was midway through creating *Hands-on Rust* when she approached me with this title. After a brief moment of shell-shock that a publisher would come to me, I accepted. Thanks are also due to all of the staff at PragProg—particularly Dave Rankin and Miki Tebeka—for letting me tweak the Brain Teasers genre a little for this title.

Thank you to Tammy Coron—the editor—for help and enthusiasm on this project. Tammy is an amazing editor, going above and beyond the call of duty by testing difficult code in the *Rust Playground* on top of keeping me focused and shepherding me through the publication process. I wouldn't have finished the book without her help.

My parents—Robert Wolverson and Dawn McLaren—deserve a lot of gratitude. They sparked my love of computers at a young age, encouraging me to experiment and learn. They are both retired teachers and instilled in me a life-long love of learning and teaching.

Kent Froeschle and Stephen Turner, my colleagues at *iZones*, get a special "thank you" for their continual encouragement, work schedule flexibility, and patiently dealing with both a global pandemic and my writing schedule.

This book would not be what it is without the patient and thorough help of the tech reviewers: Jurgis Balciunas, Forest Anderson, Vladyslav Batyrenko, Bas Zalmstra, Remco Kuijper, Andy Lester, and countless beta-readers who submitted errata and questions. Thanks are also due to Steve Cotteril, for acting as a sounding-board throughout the creative process.

Preface

Rust is a very consistent language. The Rust Core Team has worked hard to ensure that Rust does what you ask and doesn't surprise you by performing additional tasks behind your back. Rust's toolset—particularly Clippy and Rust's safety guarantees—check your program for common mistakes and often suggest improvements. It's common for Rust programmers to notice that writing their program in Rust takes a little longer, but when they run it, it works as expected.

The Rust language has a few quirks. Sometimes they creep in at the cracks between systems, and sometimes they're a conscious design choice to avoid doing something worse. In this book, you'll review a series of self-contained Rust programs that explore these quirks. Each program, known as a brain teaser, teaches an aspect of Rust that is designed to surprise you. As you read each brain teaser, try to guess the program's output correctly. The possible answers are:

- The program won't compile.

- The program produces some unexpected output (for example, "Arithmetic still works!").

- The program panics and terminates with an error message.

After each brain teaser, you'll get an explanation of why the program produces the result it does and how similar issues might affect the code you write in your own programs. To get the most out of this book, try running the code yourself *before* turning the page and reading the answer and discussion. Taking these steps helps to reinforce what you're learning. By understanding these quirks, you can become a better Rust programmer—and hopefully, avoid these pitfalls in your own projects.

About the Author

Herbert Wolverson is the author of *Hands-on Rust*,[1] and the *Rust Roguelike Tutorial*.[2] He developed and maintains the bracket-lib open source library (now part of the *Amethyst Foundation*) and has been involved in many open source projects over the years.[3] Herbert is the sole proprietor of *Bracket Productions*.

About the Code

The example projects and code are as short as possible and focused on displaying a minimal example of each brain teaser. The examples are contained within a Rust workspace. To execute each sample, change to the example's directory in your terminal and type cargo run.

Some brain teasers require additional library support. In these cases, the Cargo.toml file is displayed next to the example's source code.

About You

This book assumes that you have a working installation of Rust and that you're familiar with making and running Rust applications. Thus, the brain teasers are targeted at beginner- through intermediate-level developers. (If you're on the Rust Core Team, you probably know more about these quirks than I do.)

This book doesn't try to teach your first steps with Rust; if you've never used Rust before, start with *The Rust Programming Language [KN19]* or *Hands-on Rust [Wol21]*.[4]

Keep an Open Mind

This book exposes some of the quirks with Rust—and, sometimes, programming in general. Rust is a fantastic language despite its oddities, and these quirks aren't meant as language criticism. Instead, in many cases, you'll discover *why* things are done the way they are, making them seem less *quirky* and more *deliberate*.

As you work through this book, keep an open mind and approach each brain teaser like a crime scene investigator. All of the clues are present, and once

---

1. https://pragprog.com/titles/hwrust/hands-on-rust/
2. http://bfnightly.bracketproductions.com/rustbook/
3. https://github.com/amethyst/bracket-lib
4. https://doc.rust-lang.org/book/

you understand the discussion behind each brain teaser, you'll have a better understanding of why things work the way they do and how to avoid these particular pitfalls. You might even learn some new tricks.

If you'd like to learn more, please feel free to contact Herbert at @herberticus on Twitter or u/thebracket on Reddit.

Part I

Rust Brain Teasers

Three and a Bit

three_and_a_bit/src/main.rs
```
fn main() {
    const THREE_AND_A_BIT : f32 = 3.4028236;
    println!("{}", THREE_AND_A_BIT);
}
```

Guess the Output

 Try to guess what the output is before moving to the next page.

The program will display the following output:

```
3.4028237
```

Discussion

You might have expected the program to print 3.4028236. Surprisingly, the result is off by 0.0000001—you set a value of 3.4028236, yet the result is 3.4028237. This difference has to do with how Rust represents 32-bit floating-point numbers (the f32 type). Rust—like many other languages—represents floating-point numbers using the *IEEE-754* standard, which defines the memory layout of a float as follows:

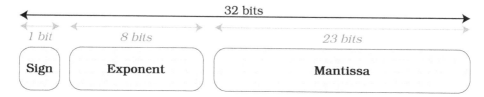

This standard also provides a formula to extract data from a floating-point variable in memory:

$$f32 = sign \text{ (-1 or 1)} \times 2^{exponent-127} \times 1.mantissa$$

Rust calculates that the most efficient way to represent 3.4028236 is to use an exponent of 2 and a mantissa of 1.7014118432998657. This is a very close approximation: 1.7014118 multiplied by 2 yields 3.4028236—the correct answer.

As it turns out, 7014118 isn't perfectly representable in 32 bits of binary. Note that the beginning of the number (1.) is assumed to exist by the IEE-754 standard but isn't actually stored. The closest representation is 7014118432998657, which introduces the following error:

$$3.4028237 = 1 \times 2^{(128-127)} \times 1.7014118432998657$$
$$3.4028237 = 3.40282368659973 14$$

The digit immediately following the 6 causes the result to be rounded up.

We're Going to Need a Bigger Float

Sometimes you can solve floating-point precision errors by using a larger floating-point type. You can represent 3.4028237 with an f64. If 64 bits aren't enough, the f128 crate can provide 128-bit floating-point numbers (at a performance cost). This isn't a panacea —some numbers are stubbornly unrepresentable as floats. Some constants such as π can't be represented by numbers at all; you're always using an approximation. Others numbers can be represented, but not cleanly as an IEE-754 float.

If you *really* need a perfect representation, Cargo includes math libraries (such as rug) that can provide arbitrary precision.[5] These libraries often carry a significant performance penalty, so consider how much precision you *need* before applying them.

How Much Precision Do You Need?

Not every program needs the same level of precision for its floating-point numbers. For example, in video games, small imprecisions in the placement of graphics usually go unnoticed. If you're working with real money, floating point errors can be disastrous (it's common to use an integer type including pennies as the last two digits, or a fixed-point library for financial calculations).

You can avoid precision issues altogether with clever design. Suppose you're designing a space-based builder game, and you want to model constructions on both Earth and Pluto. In that case, it's probably a bad idea to include both planets in the same coordinate system. Instead, you could use a "planet local" system that:

- Allows you to use much lower-precision coordinates.

- Makes it easier to account for celestial bodies' irritating habit of moving all of the time.

- Doesn't waste coordinate space on largely empty tracts of space.

As with everything in computer science, there's a trade-off between performance and accuracy. So, take a moment to think about the problem you're trying to solve with your program, and pick your numeric precision based on what you need balanced against how fast the program needs to run. Floating point numbers are directly supported by your CPU—and are very fast. Even

---

5. https://lib.rs/crates/rug

with floating point numbers, an f32 can be faster than an f64 because the 32-bit version uses less memory—you can fit more of them into your cache. Fixed-point and arbitrary precision libraries can be fast but are slower than using built-in floating point support. It's up to you to decide the accuracy/performance trade-off requirements for your programs.

Further Reading

IEE-754 Floating Point Standard:
> https://en.wikipedia.org/wiki/IEEE_754

RUG—Arbitrary Precision Numbers crate:
> https://lib.rs/crates/rug

f128 crate:
> https://lib.rs/crates/f128

fixed crate:
> https://docs.rs/fixed/1.10.0/fixed/

Non-standard Input

standard_input/src/main.rs

```rust
use std::io::stdin;

fn main() {
    println!("What is 3+2? Type your answer and press enter.");
    let mut input = String::new();
    stdin()
        .read_line(&mut input)
        .expect("Unable to read standard input");

    if input == "5" {
        println!("Correct!");
    } else {
        println!("Incorrect!");
    }
}
```

Guess the Output

 Try to guess what the output is before moving to the next page.

The program's interaction will look something like the following:

⟨ What is 3+2? Type your answer and press enter.
⟹ **5**
⟨ Incorrect!

Discussion

Normally, 3 + 2 would equal 5, but not when it comes to the way Rust handles strings. To find out why, add the following line to the end of the program:

```
println!("{:#?}", input);
```

With this new line, you're able to see the full string Rust returns from stdin:

⟨ What is 3+2? Type your answer and press enter.
⟹ **5**
⟨ Incorrect!
  "5\r\n"

Note that on UNIX-based systems, you'll see 5\n.

Rust's standard input system includes *control sequences* representing the Enter key. \r indicates a carriage return, while \n indicates a line feed. You can sanitize non-printing characters using the trim() function.

With the following program, you can correctly identify the answer to the arithmetic problem:

```rust
use std::io::stdin;

fn main() {
    println!("What is 3+2? Type your answer and press <enter>");
    let mut input = String::new();
    stdin()
        .read_line(&mut input)
        .expect("Unable to read standard input");

    if input.trim() == "5" {
        println!("Correct!");
    } else {
        println!("Incorrect!");
    }
}
```

Don't Trust Input

A good rule of thumb is to never trust input; however, there are a few things you can do to minimize your problems when input is necessary:

- When working with strings, use trim() to remove whitespace.

- When comparing strings, use to_lowercase() or to_uppercase() to ensure that you're comparing strings in the same case. These functions take care of Unicode case-folding.[6]

- When parsing complicated strings, use regular expressions to extract parts of a string.

SQL Injection

Be particularly careful with input that's passed to an SQL database or other systems that accept text commands. A malicious user might enter their name as: 10; DROP TABLE members; /*. If your program simply concatenates strings, you may end up with the following SQL getting executed on your database:

```
SELECT * FROM members WHERE id=10; DROP TABLE members; /*
```

That would be unfortunate—since the user just deleted your members database table. To help avoid this problem, you can make use of parameterized queries, which your database system should support.

Further Reading

String
https://doc.rust-lang.org/std/string/struct.String.html

trim() function
https://doc.rust-lang.org/std/string/struct.String.html#method.trim

Regex Crate
https://crates.io/crates/regex/

SQL Injection Cheat Sheet
https://www.netsparker.com/blog/web-security/sql-injection-cheat-sheet/

---

6. https://github.com/rust-lang/rust/issues/9363

Type Conversion

type_conversion/src/main.rs
```
fn main() {
    let x : u64 = 4_294_967_296;
    let y = x as u32;
    if x  == y as u64 {
        println!("x equals y.");
    } else {
        println!("x does not equal y.");
    }
}
```

Guess the Output

 Try to guess what the output is before moving to the next page.

The program will display the following output:

```
x does not equal y.
```

Discussion

Rust's as keyword is *lossy*. And when you use it to convert between types, you run the risk of losing precision without warning.

In this example, y is assigned the value 4_294_967_296, but the result is truncated because the number is greater than the maximum value of a 32-bit unsigned integer. The surprise is that neither the Rust compiler, Clippy, nor the runtime generates any kind of warning or error that data loss has occurred.

If you do plan to use the as keyword to convert between types—as most of the time Rust will perform the conversion just fine—keep the following points in mind:

- Converting a smaller type into a larger type (for example, u32 to u64) cannot lose precision, so you're safe.

- When working with numbers that are guaranteed to fit in both types, you won't lose any data. However, be careful with user submitted data or the result of calculations—if you don't control the data, you can't be *certain* that the data will be within valid ranges.

- Be careful with floating-point to integer conversions because Rust always rounds down. With that in mind, it's better to indicate the desired behavior with my_float.floor() to round down, my_float.ceil() to round up, or my_float.round() to perform normal numerical rounding. If you want rounding, perform the rounding *before* you use as.

Fortunately, Rust provides some assistance and other ways to tackle type conversion.

Literal and Non-literal Values

If you're working with *literal* values (for example, those defined directly in your source code), the Rust compiler has a knack for detecting values that won't fit in a type. For instance, have a look at the following:

```
let x: u32 = 18_446_744_073_709_551_615;
```

This code fails to compile with the error message, "the literal 18_446_744_073_709_551_615 does not fit into the type u32 whose range is 0..=4294967295."

Rust can also protect you from arithmetical errors with literal values. For example, let x = 4_294_967_295 * 2; will fail to compile.

When working with a non-literal variable (for example, user input or a calculated value), the Rust compiler can't see the values ahead of time. When you use as, you're telling Rust that you know what you're doing.

Another option is to not use as, making it easier for Rust to protect you from unexpected behavior.

Protecting Yourself Against Precision Loss

Rust provides a trait named Into to provide compile-time safe type conversions. For example, you can convert from a u32 to a u64 with the following code:

```
let y = u32::max_value();
let z: u64 = y.into();
```

Rust's Into trait resolves the problem of potentially impossible conversions by not implementing them.

The inverse of the example—converting a u64 to a u32—is impossible with Into. If you try let z : u32 = (12_u64).into(), the into() function call will fail to compile.

For conversions that may be possible, Rust provides another trait: TryInto. The following code uses try_into() to attempt to convert between a u64 and a u32:

```
use std::convert::TryInto;
let z: u32 = (5000_u64).try_into().expect("Conversion error");
```

The try_into() function returns a Result type. You can access the contents as you do with other Result types. For example, you can:

- unwrap the contents and crash if the conversion failed.
- unwrap_or to substitute a default value.
- match on the Result to handle the error explicitly.
- use expect.

The example code uses expect. If you replace 5000 with a number that won't fit into a 32-bit unsigned integer, the program crashes with a panic when it attempts the conversion.

Excessive Type Conversions

 A huge number of type conversions can be a "code smell"—an indication that something is fishy about your reasoning. If all of the functions that use x expect the value to be a u32, consider making it a u32 to begin with. If later functions require the value to be a usize, you can make your code much clearer by converting it one time rather than in each function call.

Finding Type Conversion Errors with Clippy

Rust includes a tool named *Clippy* that helps you find problems with your code. You invoke Clippy by typing cargo clippy into your terminal, which then lists the issues Clippy has found. Clippy's default settings won't find any problems with this example, but a stricter pedantic mode can notice the potential problems. To enable pedantic mode, add one line to the beginning of your main.rs file, like so:

```
#[warn(clippy::pedantic)]
```

Clippy now reports the following warnings when you run cargo clippy:

```
warning: casting `u64` to `u32` may truncate the value
warning: casting `u32` to `u64` may become silently lossy if you later
change the type
```

Pedantic-mode Clippy eagerly reports every potential error it notices—even when they aren't causing problems. Many developers find this level of reporting tiresome. Plus, pedantic checking can slow progress on large projects. A good compromise is to periodically run Clippy in pedantic mode and then comment out the change once you've digested the results.

Further Reading

"as"
   https://doc.rust-lang.org/std/keyword.as.html

"as" considered harmful?
   https://users.rust-lang.org/t/as-considered-harmful/35338

into
   https://doc.rust-lang.org/std/convert/trait.Into.html

try_into
   https://doc.rust-lang.org/std/convert/trait.TryInto.html

f32 rounding
   https://doc.rust-lang.org/std/primitive.f32.html#method.round

Byte-Sized Chunks

byte_sized/src/main.rs
```rust
fn main() {
    let mut counter : i8 = 0;
    loop {
        println!("{}", counter);
        counter += 1;
    }
}
```

Guess the Output

 Try to guess what the output is before moving to the next page.

The answer depends on how you run the program.

- If you run the program in debug mode with cargo run, the program will display a series of numbers from 0 to 127 and then crash with the following error message: thread 'main' panicked at 'attempt to add with overflow', overflow\src\main.rs:6:9.

- If you run the program in release mode with cargo run --release, the program will display a series of numbers from 0 to 127 and then from -128 to -1. It will repeat until you stop it with Ctrl+C. If you have a background in C/C++, this type of behavior is likely what you expected.

Discussion

Modern computers generally store signed integers in *two's complement*. The first bit of the number (in binary) indicates whether a number is positive (0) or negative (1). If the first bit is set, the number equals the smallest possible number for the available number of bits (-128 for an i8) *minus* the value of the other digits.

Binary arithmetic works like columnar arithmetic in base-10 (decimal); however, instead of carrying numbers larger than 10, you carry numbers larger than 1. The placement of the sign bit leads to some interesting results with two's complement arithmetic.

Look at the following two examples with a signed 8-bit integer:

- 1 + 1 = 2, as you'd expect.
- 127 + 1 = -128, because the final digit carried over, setting the sign bit.

Test in Debug Mode

Rust includes a lot of tests when debug mode is enabled that don't exist in release builds. The Rust compiler will try to help you avoid disaster, but you have to let it.

If debug mode is too slow, but you still want the added safety of overflow checks, you can enable debug mode with optimizations. To do so, add the following code to Cargo.toml:

```
[profile.dev]
opt-level = 1 # 1 for minimal optimization and good debugging.
```

Test in Debug Mode

Enabling debug optimizations will speed up your debug mode code, but your compilation times will be longer and your debugger may jump around if Rust has reordered your code—there's no such thing as a free lunch.

When You Need Overflow

Sometimes, you *want* numeric overflow to occur. Many cryptographic and random number generation algorithms assume that integer wrapping will occur. Rust lets you opt in to the behavior with the std::num::Wrapping facility. A safe version of this program looks like this:

byte_sized_wrap/src/main.rs
```
use std::num::Wrapping;

fn main() {
    let mut counter = Wrapping(0i8);
    loop {
        println!("{}", counter);
        counter += Wrapping(1i8);
    }
}
```

Detecting Overflow without Crashing

If your program doesn't need wrapping behavior, but you're concerned that you might run into a situation in which you overflow the capacity of a variable, Rust has your back. Rust's numeric types implement a series of checked functions: checked_add, checked_div, checked_mul, checked_sub, and a few others.[7]

The checked functions return an Option that will either contain Some(x) if the operation succeeded or None if an overflow occurred, as shown in this example:

```
if let Some(n) = x.checked_add(b) {
    // It worked, n contains the result.
} else {
    // Overflow occurred - handle the error.
}
```

Finally, you can combine Wrapping behavior with detection using the overflowing_ functions. These functions return a tuple that contains the result, *including* the overflow, and a bool indicating whether or not wrapping occurred.[8]

---

7. https://doc.rust-lang.org/std/primitive.u32.html#method.checked_add
8. https://doc.rust-lang.org/std/primitive.u32.html#method.overflowing_add

Further Reading

std::num::Wrapping

https://doc.rust-lang.org/std/num/struct.Wrapping.html

Two's Complement

https://en.wikipedia.org/wiki/Two%27s_complement

Cargo Profiles

https://doc.rust-lang.org/cargo/reference/profiles.html

Rust Data Types

https://doc.rust-lang.org/book/ch03-02-data-types.html

How Long Is a String?

string_length/src/main.rs
```rust
const HELLO_WORLD : &'static str = "Halló heimur";

fn main() {
    println!("{} is {} characters long.",
        HELLO_WORLD,
        HELLO_WORLD.len()
    );
}
```

Guess the Output

 Try to guess what the output is before moving to the next page.

The program will display the following output:

```
Halló heimur is 13 characters long.
```

Discussion

Your eyes aren't deceiving you—"Halló heimur", contains 12 characters (including the space). Let's step back and take a look at how Rust's String type works. The internal struct definition of a String is straightforward:

```
pub struct String {
    vec: Vec<u8>,
}
```

Strings are just a vector of bytes (u8), representing Unicode characters in an encoding named UTF-8. Rust automatically translates your string to UTF-8. The encoding looks like this:

H a l l ó h e i m u r Unicode Characters (10 characters)

0x48 0x64 0x6C 0xC6 0xC3 0x20 0x68 0x65 0x69 0x6D 0x75 0x72
0xB3 UTF-8 Encoding: Scalar Values (19 bytes)

Your original string, "Halló heimur" consists of 11 ASCII characters (including the space) and one Latin-1 Supplement character: the ó. ASCII characters require 1 byte to encode, Latin supplements require 2 bytes.

Rust's string encoding is smart enough to not store extra zeroes for each Unicode character. If it did, String would be a vector of char types. Rust's char is exactly 4 bytes long—the *maximum* size of a single Unicode character.[9] Char variables don't represent a single ASCII character; instead, they represent a *Unicode scalar value*. The scalar value can represent a single glyph or modification to another glyph.

String Length

String.len() counts the number of bytes in the string's backing vector. If a String was storing every character as a char, you'd expect Halló heimur to occupy 48 bytes of memory. Rust's String isn't storing characters; it's storing a byte array representing just the bytes needed to output the stored text.

---

9. https://doc.rust-lang.org/std/primitive.char.html#representation

Not all UTF-8 characters require all 4 bytes to render. For example, a space requires only 1 byte (0x20), while most Latin Extension characters use 2 bytes. The first byte (0xC3) indicates that the character uses the Latin Extension character region, and the second byte (0xB3 for ó) identifies the character.

The string Halló heimur contains 11 ASCII characters—each using 1 byte of memory—and occupies 11 bytes. Add 2 bytes for the ó and your string occupies 13 bytes of memory.

Counting Characters

You can correctly count the characters in Halló heimur with the following code:

```
println!("{} is {} characters long.",
    HELLO_WORLD,
    HELLO_WORLD
        .chars() // Convert to an iterator over a char sequence
        .count() // Count the characters in the sequence
);
```

When you call my_str.chars(), you're requesting an iterator that returns each element of the string represented as a char.[10] Rust correctly deduces that there are a total of 12 glyphs—or Unicode scalar values—making up the string. The iterator passes each of them to your consumer as a 4-byte char. Even if a glyph only requires 1 or 2 bytes of memory, Rust will allocate all 4 bytes for the char type. Traversing the iterator uses very little extra memory. If you call collect() on the iterator—to create a vector of char data—the vector will consume 40 bytes of memory.

Use my_str.chars() to access individual characters in a String. It's an iterator, so you can use nth, for_each and other iterator functions to find what you're looking for. For example, you can access the fourth character in a string with my_str.chars().nth(4).

Impact of UTF-8 Sizing

Unicode string sizing can be confusing at times, which can lead to surprising results in your code. You need to be aware of the distinction between characters and bytes:

- When you're validating string length, know what counts and what doesn't. For example, if you only accept usernames that are 10 characters or less, you need to decide if you mean glyphs or bytes.

---

10. https://doc.rust-lang.org/std/str/struct.Chars.html

- When storing strings in databases, you need to remember to allocate enough space for non-English character set strings.

- When transmitting or receiving information to/from a remote API, you need to agree on a length standard for encoding strings in transit.

- If you're writing a program for a memory constrained system, parsing Unicode string character by character can consume a *lot* more memory than you expected. The string love: ♥ is 7 characters long, requires 12 bytes of storage in a String—and 32 bytes of memory when processed as individual characters. This may seem like a small amount of memory, but if your reader enters the entirety of *War and Peace* into your program's input box, per-character parsing may require more resources than you expected.

- When accessing individual characters in a string, it's much safer to use chars as opposed to directly accessing the byte array. Characters are aware of Unicode boundaries—bytes are not. Printing the first 6 bytes of "Können" will only print "Könne". Printing the first 6 characters will output the entire word.

Further Reading

Char
>   https://doc.rust-lang.org/std/primitive.char.html

String length
>   https://doc.rust-lang.org/std/string/struct.String.html#method.len

Unicode Symbol Reference
>   https://www.compart.com/en/unicode/

Wikipedia UTF-8
>   https://en.wikipedia.org/wiki/UTF-8

String Source Code
>   https://doc.rust-lang.org/src/alloc/string.rs.html

Please Reboot the Universe

reboot_universe/src/main.rs
```rust
fn main() {
    if 0.1 + 0.2 == 0.3 {
        println!("Arithmetic still works.");
    } else {
        println!("Please reboot the universe.");
    }
}
```

Guess the Output

 Try to guess what the output is before moving to the next page.

The program will display the following output:

```
Please reboot the universe.
```

Discussion

You would expect 0.1 + 0.2 to equal 0.3—it does, but not in floating-point math. The answer is *really* close, but the floating-point approximations prevent the comparison from succeeding as if the arithmetic no longer works. This scenario is related to the previous teaser, Puzzle 1, Three and a Bit, on page 3.

As you might have guessed by now, floating-point comparison is fraught with errors—errors that may not be so obvious at first glance.

Consider a long-running program that checks to see if it's done by examining the floating-point product of some calculation, or perhaps you've got a series of unit tests that meticulously checks your math functions against known-good answers. In both cases, the calculated values may not be "close enough" to correct to make things work as expected. In other words, the program may never terminate, and the tests may fail—even when they shouldn't.

Because the build-up of tiny errors can lead to much larger problems, many computer science teachers tell their students to "never compare floats."

Use Clippy to Help Catch Mistakes

Thankfully, you can use Clippy (Rust's linter) to help spot problems before they arise.

To see Clippy in action with this brain teaser, invoke Clippy by typing `cargo clippy` in the `code/float_compare` example directory.

Clippy will produce the following warning:

```
| ^^^^^^^^^^^^^^^^^ help: consider comparing them within some margin of error:
| `(0.1 + 0.2 - 0.3).abs() < error_margin`
= note: `#[deny(clippy::float_cmp)]` on by default
= note: `f32::EPSILON` and `f64::EPSILON` are available for the `error_margin`
  help: for further information visit
  https://rust-lang.github.io/rust-clippy/master/index.html#float_cmp
```

As a bonus, Clippy offers a safe alternative to the comparison. If you include floating-point precision limits in your comparison, you can safely compare floats and ensure that they're "close enough" to the answer you wanted.

Clippy also suggests using EPSILON as a margin of error. EPSILON is built-in to each of Rust's floating-point types. You can restore your faith in Rust's arithmetic skills using the following code:

```
if (0.1f32 + 0.2f32 - 0.3f32).abs() < std::f32::EPSILON {
    println!("Arithmetic works");
}
```

Comparison with EPSILON can be unwieldy. The float_cmp crate provides a convenient interface for calculating approximate equality with the approx_eq! macro.[11]

Beware of External Libraries

Be especially careful when you're interacting with floating-point results from external libraries. If they were compiled with the C fastmath extension, they might be even more inaccurate than you expected. Fastmath takes some liberties with calculations in the name of speed, providing answers that are very close to what you need but not quite there. In some cases, fastmath may or may not even elect to apply an optimization—if precision is important, try to find a version of an external library that doesn't use this optimization.

My team recently ported some radio frequency calculations from an old C++ library to Rust. Despite using EPSILON, our unit tests kept failing. After much head-scratching, we discovered that the library we'd been using for nearly a decade was inaccurate beyond four decimal places. The funny thing was: it didn't matter at all because we never needed that much precision. We used float_cmp with a larger error margin to demonstrate that our ported code was close enough to the known-good values we had from the old library and carried on.

Further Reading

float-cmp crate
    https://crates.io/crates/float-cmp

Float Comparison Warning from Clippy
    https://rust-lang.github.io/rust-clippy/master/index.html#float_cmp

---

11. https://crates.io/crates/float-cmp

There and Back Again

there_and_back/src/main.rs

```rust
use std::f32::consts::PI;

pub struct Degrees(pub f32);
pub struct Radians(pub f32);

impl Degrees {
    pub fn new(angle: f32) -> Self {
        Self(angle)
    }
}

impl From<Degrees> for Radians {
    fn from(item : Degrees) -> Self {
        Self(item.0 * PI / 180.0)
    }
}

fn main() {
    let one_eighty_degrees = Degrees::new(180.0);
    let one_eighty_radians : Radians = one_eighty_degrees.into();
    println!("180 Degrees in Radians = {}", one_eighty_radians.0);
}
```

Guess the Output

Try to guess what the output is before moving to the next page.

The program will display the following output:

```
180 Degrees in Radians = 3.1415927
```

Discussion

The surprise here is that the *Into* trait wasn't implemented, yet the program was still able to use the into() function with the Radians type.

When you define the From trait, Rust automatically implements the reciprocal Into trait for you. This is very convenient—and also surprising, given Rust's general insistence on behavior being defined explicitly. Prior to Rust version 1.4.1, this automatic implementation was only performed for types accessible from the crate that defines the type; newer releases always include the reciprocal.

Using the example code from this brain teaser, you can convert degrees to radians using either let r : Radians = d.into() or let r = Radians::from(d). This conversion works because Rust added into() to the Degrees type, and the program already defined from(). However, because Rust didn't add the reverse conversion, nor did the program, you need to add the following code to convert from radians to degrees:

```
impl From<Radians> for Degrees {
    fn from(item: Radians) -> Self {
        Self(item.0 / (PI / 180.0))
    }
}
```

Adding this code allows you to convert between degrees and radians—and then back again. Rust doesn't automatically implement the conversion in both directions because sometimes it only makes sense to convert one way. You can turn an egg into an omelette, but it's not so easy to turn an omelette into an egg. The same can be true of data types. If a conversion loses any data, Rust has no way of knowing what values it should insert into every field of your destination type.

Failing on Impossible Conversions

As you saw in Puzzle 3, Type Conversion, on page 11, not every conversion works. But don't worry, you can implement your own TryFrom trait for your types to provide conversion with the possibility of reporting failure.

Suppose you want to constrain a numeric type to only accept values between 0 and 10; you might do something like this to implement try_from:

```
use std::convert::TryFrom;

struct ZeroToTen(i32);

impl TryFrom<i32> for ZeroToTen {
    type Error = &'static str;

    fn try_from(value: i32) -> Result<Self, Self::Error> {
        if value < 0 || value > 10 {
            Err("Value must be between 0 and 10")
        } else {
            Ok(Self(value))
        }
    }
}
```

Just like the From trait, defining TryFrom automatically creates a reciprocal Try-Into for you.

Use Strong Types to Reduce Bugs

Suppose you're working with different units of measurement, like meters, feet, inches, and centimeters. To reduce the potential mistake of an inches to centimeters conversion, you can define the units of measurement and the conversions between them. Then, when you perform a calculation that requires a unit of measure, you can define the unit type in the function's parameters.

Some languages—notably Ada—let you limit types to a certain range. This range limitation is helpful in cases where a value should never fall outside of the defined range. By defining a range-limited type, you can automatically include this test whenever type-conversion is performed.

Strong types can help transform logical errors—such as using degrees when you meant radians—into compile-time errors, leading to fewer bugs in your code.

Further Reading

std::convert::From trait
    https://doc.rust-lang.org/std/convert/trait.From.html

std::convert::TryFrom trait
    https://doc.rust-lang.org/std/convert/trait.TryFrom.html

Walks Like a Duck, Quacks Like a Duck

quack/src/main.rs
```rust
fn double_it(n: u64, _: i32) -> u64 {
    n * 2
}

fn main() {
    let one: i32 = 1;
    let n = double_it(one as _, 3);
    println!("{}", n);
}
```

Guess the Output

Try to guess what the output is before moving to the next page.

The program will display the following output, showing no warnings or errors:

2

Discussion

We find two surprises:

- You can name a function parameter _, requiring users of that function to send a variable in that parameter location. The variable will never be used and will instead get *optimized away* in release builds.

- one as _ compiles and works. The i32 was converted to a u64 without having to specify a type.

Rust doesn't support *duck typing*—automatic conversion between types if any similar type is available—and is generally very strict about type conversions.

Rust's underscore (or *placeholder*) symbol has different meanings in different contexts:

- When used as a variable name prefix (for example, _ignore_me : i32), the underscore indicates to Rust that the variable is deliberately unused and suppresses "unused variable" warnings.

- When used as an entire variable name, you're telling Rust that you never intend to use the variable. When used in a match statement (for example, _ => { .. }), the underscore indicates a default action. If no other match branch is selected, then the default action will be evaluated.

- Underscores can be used with functions that return a value marked with #[must_use]. For example, let _ = my_important_function() will ignore the result of the function, suppressing errors or warnings that you're not using the result.

When used with an as keyword, _ indicates that Rust should try to convert the value into whatever type is expected in this context. For example, function_that_requires_a_u32(x as _) will try to convert x—irrespective of its type—to a u32. If x is of a type that can never be converted to a u32, the Rust compiler will stop with an error. If it's a type that *might* be convertible, Rust will try and convert it—with the same potential precision-loss issues you saw in Puzzle 7, There and Back Again, on page 27.

This is called *inferred typing*. Rust will try to *infer* the desired type of a variable from the context in which it's used. In the example, the function requires a u64, so Rust tries to convert your variable into a 64-bit unsigned integer.

Inferred typing can be a very helpful shorthand, especially with complex type names, but you shouldn't use it everywhere.

Why Not Use Inferred Typing Everywhere?

It's very tempting to use as _ everywhere in your code and stop worrying about type conversions. Most of the time, this will work—subject to data truncation. So why wouldn't you want to do this?

The Rust documentation is clear that the language doesn't want you to use as _ everywhere:

> as can also be used with the _ placeholder when the destination type can be inferred. Note that this can cause inference breakage and usually such code should use an explicit type for both clarity and stability.[12]

The disadvantages to using as _ may be summarized as follows:

- Using clearly named types—and naming them clearly—can make the intent of your code much easier to deduce. Even if you're working alone, when you return to the project after several weeks, it can be difficult to remember what you were thinking when you wrote x as _.

- Sometimes, Rust's type inference breaks when chains of variables need to have their types inferred.

- Many development environments will struggle to show you the concrete type of variables after inferred conversion.

- You can introduce subtle bugs if Rust's type inference decides that a type will work and it isn't the type you were expecting.

So even though Rust is tempting you with a duck typing solution, it usually isn't a great idea to use it all the time. When you combine type inference issues with the potential precision loss from the as keyword, you're inviting trouble. In many cases, you should use into() (or try_into()) instead of as altogether.

When Should You Use Inferred Typing?

The most common use-case for as _ is low-level pointer code. The following code clones a type and returns it as a pointer:

---

12. https://doc.rust-lang.org/std/keyword.as.html

```
unsafe fn clone_ptr(&self) -> *mut () {
    Box::into_raw(Box::new(self.clone())) as _
}
```

You don't often need to do this, but when you do, as _ helps simplify some already difficult-to-read code. It's also common to encounter as _ in libraries that are still in early development. The library developers may not be certain what type an interface will use yet, so examples with as _ are common until the API is stabilized.

Converting Types in Real Code

In larger programs, it's inevitable that you will have to convert between types. You can use as _ when Rust can be certain of the desired type—but it isn't recommended as your first port of call. Generally, try to favor type conversions in the following order of preference:

1. Using into() is precise and optimizes very well.
2. try_into() lets you handle failed conversions.
3. Use as type when you are certain that conversions are safe.
4. Use as _ when you are really stuck.

Further Reading

Underscore
> https://runrust.miraheze.org/wiki/Underscore

As
> https://doc.rust-lang.org/std/keyword.as.html

Out of Order

out_of_order/src/main.rs

```
fn main() {
    let mut floats = vec![3.1, 1.2, 4.5, 0.3];
    floats.sort();

    println!("{:#?}", floats);
}
```

Guess the Output

 Try to guess what the output is before moving to the next page.

The program will fail to compile, and you'll receive the following error message:

```
the trait `Ord` is not implemented for `{float}`
```

Discussion

Rust makes it easy to sort vectors of most types. A vector's sort() function can sort a vector of strings alphabetically or a vector of integers numerically without issue. So why doesn't sorting a vector of floating-point numbers work? Since floating-point numbers aren't always *numbers* (more on that in a minute), they aren't always naturally sortable. Rust generally makes sorting values easy, but it's also careful to avoid implicit behavior that can surprise the programmer.

Consider the following "impossible" math calculations:

- The tangent of 90° is infinity, so there's no appropriate result.
- Dividing by zero yields infinity or negative infinity.
- Comparing infinity with infinity doesn't make sense.
- Comparing non-number floats with *anything* also doesn't make any sense.

In each example, the result is *not* a number. To make calculations like this possible, floating-point numbers can also store Not a Number (NaN) and Infinity.

Rust introduced the PartialOrd and PartialEq traits—and the accompanying partial_cmp() function—to represent numeric types that are generally comparable but may feature cases in which two numbers cannot be naturally compared or ordered.

tan(90°)

The tangent of 90° is NaN. Entertainingly, floating-point inaccuracies make demonstrating this difficult:

```
println!("{}", (90.0 * (std::f32::consts::PI/180.0)).tan());
```

This snippet prints -22877334.0. The conversion of 90° to radians has lost precision, resulting in an angle that *does* have a tangent.

Rust's floating-point number supports both PartialOrd and PartialEq, so they *can* be sorted, but not with the same syntax as other types.

Safely Sorting Floats

You *can* sort a vector of floats using the following code:

```
let mut floats = vec![3.1, 1.2, 4.5, 0.3];
floats.sort_by(|a, b| a.partial_cmp(b).unwrap());
```

The partial_cmp function (provided via the PartialOrd trait) returns an Option. You can access the contained ordering information by calling unwrap on the result. Unwrapping an empty option will crash your program if the value could not be ordered—because an INFINITY or NaN snuck into your data.

If you're sure that you won't be dealing with invalid floating-point numbers, you can simply unwrap() the results of partial_cmp and use that to sort your data in the sort_by() function.

If your code might encounter an invalid value, you can use unwrap_or to provide a default sort order for invalid numbers:

```
use std::cmp::Ordering::Less;
let mut floats = vec![
  3.1, 1.2, 4.5, 0.3, std::f32::INFINITY, std::f32::NAN
];
floats.sort_by(|a, b| a.partial_cmp(b).unwrap_or(Less));
```

The even longer sort_by call works and is safe with invalid numbers, but it's a lot of code to type whenever you need to sort a slice of floating-point numbers. To help solve this problem, here's a handy function you can keep in your toolbox to simplify this process:

```
fn float_sort<T : PartialOrd>(data: &mut [T]) {
    use std::cmp::Ordering::Less;
    data.sort_by(|a, b| a.partial_cmp(b).unwrap_or(Less));
}
```

You can then use the float_sort function to safely sort any slice (collection of numbers, typically the contents of an array or vector) of floating-point numbers:

```
let mut floats = vec![
  3.1, 1.2, 4.5, 0.3, std::f32::INFINITY, std::f32::NAN
];
float_sort(&mut floats);
```

What Do You Mean, Slice?

Slice is Rust-ese for the contents of a container. A vector or array containing [1,2,3] can refer to the contents as a slice without having to know how the container works.

Further Reading

Ord trait

https://doc.rust-lang.org/std/cmp/trait.Ord.html

PartialOrd trait

https://doc.rust-lang.org/std/cmp/trait.PartialOrd.html

f32 primitive

https://doc.rust-lang.org/std/primitive.f32.html

X Marks the Spot

x_marks_spot/src/main.rs

```rust
fn main() {
    if 'X' == 'X' {
        println!("It matches!");
    } else {
        println!("It doesn't match.");
    }
}
```

Guess the Output

 Try to guess what the output is before moving to the next page.

The program will display the following output:

```
It doesn't match.
```

Discussion

Unicode allows for *homoglyphs*, which are very similar or identical characters that can be encoded in different ways. The first X is the Latin Unicode character, encoded as 0x58. The second X is the Greek capital letter Chi, encoded in UTF-8 as 0xCE 0xA7. If you look closely, they aren't identical, but in some fonts—notably Consolas on Windows—they are indistinguishable.

Homoglyphs are popular in *phishing* attacks. The domain name bertbank.com may look like it's innocently asking you to change your password, but the e is actually Cyrillic (0xD0 0xB5). You're not in the habit of handing over your login details to a fake bank, but it's not so easy to see the fake domain name at first glance.

Homoglyph Help Is on the Way

A Rust compiler warning is currently in development to help you identify when you're using confusingly similar characters in your code.[13] It isn't perfect, but when this compiler feature is complete, it'll generate a warning when you compile your code. You can also use the Nettfiske crate to detect likely obfuscations in text.

A second surprising effect of homoglyphs relates to string length. X requires only a single byte inside of a String (it's still 4 bytes long as a char). The Cyrillic X is 2 bytes long. You should be careful to either sanitize user input length to expected values or be sufficiently flexible to handle input from users with non-English keyboards.

Multi-Glyph Homoglyphs

Just in case you weren't already confused, UTF-8 introduces *another* way to generate the same character. Some Unicode characters serve to modify the output of the next or previous character in the string. For example, you can express Mañana using the Latin Small Letter N with Tilde (0xC3 0xB1), or you can express it as man\u{0303}ana using the UTF-8 symbol 0x0303. The 0x0303 symbol applies a tilde to the previous character, the n.

---

13. https://rust-lang.github.io/rfcs/2457-non-ascii-idents.html

This is especially problematic if you modify the string. For example, reversing mañana with the Latin character correctly gives anañam. Using the same .chars().rev().collect() to reverse the version with the modifier incorrectly gives you anãnam—the tilde is in the wrong place. The unicode-reverse crate can help with this particular case, but you need to be extra careful when editing UTF-8 strings because of this problem.

Modifier characters are often used to enter crazy-looking text on forums such as Reddit. The following examples are all in a sans-serif font, but they use UTF-8 modifiers to adjust the text:

Further Reading

Wikipedia Homoglyphs
https://en.wikipedia.org/wiki/Homoglyph

Homoglyph Attack Generator
https://www.irongeek.com/homoglyph-attack-generator.php

Nettfiske—Homoglyph Detector Crate
https://crates.io/crates/nettfiske

Unicode Reverse Crate
https://crates.io/crates/unicode-reverse

Weird Text Generator
https://lingojam.com/WeirdTextGenerator

Stacking Boxes

boxes/src/main.rs
```
fn main() {
    let c = Box::new([0u32; 10_000_000]);
    println!("{}", c.len());
}
```

Guess the Output

 Try to guess what the output is before moving to the next page.

In debug mode, the program will crash with the message thread 'main' has overflowed its stack. In release mode, the program will display the following output: 10000000.

Discussion

10,000,000 32-bit integers requires 40Mb of memory to store—larger than the default stack. Attempting to get around this limitation, the code uses Box to place the structure on the heap. However, in debug mode, Rust first allocates the array on the stack and then moves it to the heap, crashing the program.

To better understand the example, let's look at how program memory is arranged. Computer programs use two distinct areas of memory while operating: the *stack* and the *heap*.

What Is the Stack?

Every program running on your computer maintains its own stack—a small resource that uses 2 megabytes per thread by default.[14] Stacks are intentionally kept small for better performance.

Because the stack is small, it's likely to fit entirely inside your CPU's memory cache. Your program runs faster, and the stack remains "hot"—unlikely to be evicted from cache or paged into virtual memory.

The stack stores local variables, function parameters, and the *call stack*—a list of functions your program has called, and the point to which execution should return when a function finishes execution.

Stacks are considered *LIFO*—last in, first out. To better understand this concept, think of a stack like a pile of dinner plates. The last plate you add to the pile is the first plate you can access later on. Adding an element to the stack is known as *pushing*, whereas removing the topmost element from the stack is known as *popping*.

The stack sees constant use while your program runs:

- Whenever you create a local variable (a variable that exists only in the current scope), the variable gets pushed to the stack. Local variables can be references, in which case the *reference* is stored on the stack—but the referred-to data may be anywhere.

---

14. https://doc.rust-lang.org/std/thread/

- Whenever you leave a scope, the scope's variables are popped from the stack.

- Whenever you call a function, the parameters to the function are pushed to the stack, along with the memory address to which the function should return when its operation is complete.

The stack also provides a handy debugging tool. Every function call is pushed to the stack; if your program crashes, Rust *walks* the stack to show you a stack trace describing the state of your program when it crashed.

What Is the Heap?

The heap—another area of memory that every program maintains—is limited by your computer's available memory, virtual memory, and operating system limitations. Heap memory is large and may or may not be contiguous, depending upon your operating system.

Storing data on the heap requires more steps than storing data on the stack. First, Rust's standard library needs to request a heap allocation that returns a pointer to a usable area of memory. It then needs to store the pointer before it can write data to the heap.

Reading data from the heap also requires a little more work: to read data, your program first needs to read the pointer to determine where the heap data is stored. Once it knows the location, the program can read the data from there.

Because of the extra steps required for heap read/write access—particularly with frequent allocations—accessing data on the heap can be a lot slower than accessing data on the stack. Why? Because the CPU's memory cache will try its best to keep your heap data available—but heap-allocated data is often large and is more likely to be evicted from the cache than the program's stack. The heap is also less likely to be contiguous in memory than the stack, making cache misses more likely.

Most of Rust's container types automatically use the heap. For example, the Vec type is defined as follows:[15]

```
pub struct Vec<T, A: Allocator = Global> {
    buf: RawVec<T, A>,
    len: usize,
}
```

---

15. https://doc.rust-lang.org/src/alloc/vec/mod.rs.html

A vector is just a pointer to an area of memory (abstracted inside RawVec) and the length of the stored data.

Now that you understand the differences between the stack and the heap, let's consider some strategies for storing large data structures on the heap.

Storing Large Blocks of Data on the Heap

The Box type represents a smart pointer to heap memory, making it a natural way to store large arrays on the heap. Unfortunately, constructing a box with Box::new *first* creates the array on the stack and then moves it to the heap. This process causes your stack to overflow and the program to crash.

Several methods ensure that data is stored on the heap, solving the issue in this example:

- Replace your array with a Vec, which automatically uses the heap.
- Use Box to wrap a pointer to the heap.
- Use compiler optimizations to avoid the issue in this example.

Let's start by not using arrays at all.

Solving Stack Overflow with Vectors

You can avoid exhausting stack memory by using a Vec instead of an array. Vectors always allocate their contents on the heap, allowing much larger data sets to be safely used. The following code allocates memory directly to the heap in a vector:

```
#[feature(box_syntax)]
fn main() {
    let x = vec![0u32; 10_000_000];
}
```

Stack vs. Heap in Other Languages

Readers coming from C, C++, or other systems languages will have encountered similar problems. The stack is a finite resource in most languages, and its usage for large data-structures should be weighed carefully. In C, you may solve the problem by using malloc to allocate an area of memory for your data structure. In C++, new or a smart pointer provides the same service. Just like Box, you're allocating to the heap instead of the stack.

Using a Vec adds a small amount of overhead—the size of the vector is stored. If you don't extend your vector once it's created, it otherwise performs exactly the same as an array allocated on the

Stack vs. Heap in Other Languages

heap in other languages. Rust also gives you overflow detection in debug-mode builds (and elides them in optimized builds), giving you extra development safety—and no speed overhead in a release build. Using Vec instead of an array is a very small price to pay for the additional memory safety Rust brings to the table.

Using a vector wastes a few bytes of memory (storing the size) but provides equivalent operation. In most cases, this is "good enough." However, if you have your heart set on using an array, the compiler can help you out.

Solving Stack Overflow with Compiler Optimizations

When you run the example in release mode, the program works fine. This is because LLVM (the compiler engine underneath Rust) is smart enough to detect an allocation being immediately moved to the heap and skips the stack allocation altogether. However, there are two problems with relying on this optimization:

1. You can't always be 100% certain the optimization will be applied; it usually will, but compilers aren't perfect.

2. You can't run your program in debug mode anymore.

Relying on the compiler to save the day can work, but it's not optimal. The Rust Core Team is aware of the issue and is working to resolve it. A new Box syntax—not yet stabilized in mainline Rust—can solve the entire problem.

Solving Stack Overflow with Nightly/Unstable Rust

You can also make use of the proposed box_syntax feature, but it's not yet stabilized in core Rust. There's general agreement on the need for box syntax, and little progress in stabilizing it—so it's unclear when/if this feature will be promoted to stable Rust. The following code uses the *proposed* Box syntax to allocate directly to the heap:

```
#[feature(box_syntax)]
fn main() {
    let x = box [0; 10_000_000];
}
```

The new Box syntax is currently available only in the unstable branch of Rust. Using unstable features requires that you enable the nightly Rust toolchain. If you'd like to default to the nightly toolchain—which isn't always perfectly stable—you can switch your default with rustup:

```
rustup default nightly
```

You can also compile your program with Cargo, using an additional command-line flag:

```
cargo +nightly run
```

Unstable Isn't Stable

nightly offers many upcoming Rust features, including ones that won't make it to the stable channel. Nightly features may change, and can even vanish. Use them at your own risk.

Also, a beta channel provides access to nearly stable features scheduled for inclusion in the main compiler.

At some point, Rust will stabilize the new Box syntax. Until then, your choices aren't all that great: you can replace your array with a Vec, rely on the compiler, or use not-yet-stabilized syntax. Of those choices, Vec is probably the best because vectors are very stable, operate like arrays, and perform very well.

Further Reading

The Stack and the Heap
>   https://doc.rust-lang.org/1.22.0/book/first-edition/the-stack-and-the-heap.html

Box Type
>   https://doc.rust-lang.org/std/boxed/struct.Box.html

box_syntax
>   https://doc.rust-lang.org/beta/unstable-book/language-features/box-syntax.html

Amnesia

amnesia/src/main.rs

```rust
fn main() {
    loop {
        let buffer = (0..1000).collect::<Vec<u32>>();
        std::mem::forget(buffer);
        print!(".");
    }
}
```

Guess the Output

Try to guess what the output is before moving to the next page.

The program will display the following output, forever:

.

Discussion

The program running endlessly isn't surprising since the program loops forever without a break to stop the loop. The surprise comes when you let it run for a while as it eventually consumes all of your computer's memory or is terminated by your operating system. Allocating memory, losing the reference to it, and never cleaning up after yourself is known as a *memory leak*.

Equally surprising is that Rust generally makes you wrap violations of memory safety guarantees in unsafe tags; however, no unsafe tags are shown in this example.

Rust makes strong—compiler-guaranteed—promises regarding memory safety. Yet, surprisingly, memory leaks are not a violation of memory safety. In fact, Rust even provides std::mem::forget and Box::leak to let you explicitly cause a memory leak.

Memory Leaks Are Safe?

The forget function used to be marked as unsafe, but the Rust Core Team decided that memory leaks fall outside of Rust's memory protection guarantee. Huon Wilson (Rust Core Team Alumni) summarizes Rust's philosophy on memory leaks as follows:

> Put simply: memory unsafety is doing something with invalid data, a memory leak is not doing something with valid data.[16]

The Rust documentation adds to this statement:

> forget is not marked as unsafe, because Rust's safety guarantees do not include a guarantee that destructors will always run. For example, a program can create a reference cycle using Rc, or call process::exit to exit without running destructors. Thus, allowing mem::forget from safe code does not fundamentally change Rust's safety guarantees.[17]

Rust provides two ways to stop using a variable:

---

16. http://huonw.github.io/blog/2016/04/memory-leaks-are-memory-safe/
17. https://doc.rust-lang.org/std/mem/fn.forget.html

The first is to use std::mem::drop as it guarantees that any destructors—implemented with the Drop trait—will get executed. Using std::mem::drop generally cleans up memory and is the preferred approach. With std::mem::drop, or when a variable leaves scope, any Drop destructors are executed for you.

The other approach is to use std::mem::forget, which skips the destructor and simply "forgets" the reference to the area of memory that the forgotten variable is pointing to. With std::mem::forget, the forgotten variable is still allocated and using memory.

Despite memory leaks being safe, Rust does help you avoid them.

Rust Does Help Prevent Leaks

In normal usage, Rust helps you avoid memory leaks by default. When a variable "drops" out of scope, it's drop destructor is automatically called. The following code drops the vector when the scope exits:

```
{
  let my_vec = vec![100; 100];
}
```

The previous code is functionally equivalent to the following code:

```
let my_vec = vec![100; 100];
std::mem::drop(my_vec);
```

In both cases, the vector's destructor is called. For a vector, this safely deletes the allocated buffer and remembers to call drop on every stored item. Automatic cleanup is provided by all of Rust's built-in collection types. Likewise, Rust's built-in variable types clean up after themselves. In most cases, any type you create will do the same, but if you need to explicitly release any resources, you can always implement the Drop trait.

Many Rust programs don't need to worry about memory management beyond letting Rust destroy variables when they leave scope. If you need more control, Rust provides smart pointer types.

Smart Pointers

A common way of creating a pointer to the heap is to embed your variable in a Box. Boxes are *smart pointers*, similar to unique_ptr in C++. A Box contains a pointer to its contents and implements Drop to ensure the pointer is deleted as soon as your Box goes out of scope. Unless you explicitly call leak or forget on the Box, it's guaranteed to be correctly removed from memory for you.

Rust also includes an analogue to C++'s shared_ptr, which is a reference-counted pointer. The Rc type wraps data in a pointer and increases the reference count when it's cloned. Rc decreases the reference count when dropped, destroying the entire structure and its contents if the reference count reaches zero.

Rust also provides Arc, which is an *atomic* reference-counted smart pointer. Atomic variables automatically provide thread-safe access. Arc works similarly to regular reference-counted pointers, but it's safe to use in a multithreaded environment. Tasks can concurrently increase or decrease the reference count without crashing your program or creating a data race.

Rust provides the tools you need to not leak memory—so why does it provide the option? Sometimes you need Rust to stop managing an area of memory.

Sometimes You Need to Forget

Most experienced developers will tell you that deliberately leaking memory is a bad idea. But there are times that you need to forget a variable. For example, you might be passing control over an area of memory or control handle to another program and require that Rust not delete it.

For example, if you've opened a file handle (with File::open) and immediately pass that handle to another application, you need to forget the handle so that your program doesn't close the handle, invalidating the second program's access.

Another example is interoperability with another program. You might allocate an area of memory—possibly in a specific location for interprocess memory sharing—and then you want to hand control of that memory over to another program. You don't want Rust to clean the memory for you, because it's now the responsibility of the recipient program. The other program may not even be written in Rust—forget is often found in C interoperability code for this reason.[18]

std::mem::forget is a powerful tool but one that must be used with extreme care. If you don't have a very specific need for it, it's best not to forget your memory.

Further Reading

std::mem::Forget
> https://doc.rust-lang.org/std/mem/fn.forget.html

std::boxed::Box
> https://doc.rust-lang.org/std/boxed/struct.Box.html

---

18. https://www.ralphminderhoud.com/blog/rust-ffi-wrong-way/

Reverse the Polarity of the Neutron Flow

reverse_polarity/src/main.rs
```rust
fn display_neutron_flow(polarity: isize) {
    println!(
        "Neutron Flow is {}",
        if polarity < 0 { "reversed"} else { "normal" }
    );
}

fn main() {
    let polarity = 1;
    {
        let polarity = polarity - 2;
        display_neutron_flow(polarity);
    }
    display_neutron_flow(polarity);
}
```

Guess the Output

 Try to guess what the output is before moving to the next page.

The program will display the following output:

```
Neutron Flow is reversed
Neutron Flow is normal
```

Discussion

The code creates a variable named polarity. It then creates *another* variable with the same name and a different value. Reusing variable names is known as *shadowing* and is a controversial topic in Rust development houses. Rust explicitly permits the creation of shadowed variables; however, unlike many other languages, you won't see a compiler warning when using this feature.

Let's take a step back and look at what let polarity = 1; *really* does. With this code, the compiler:

1. Sets aside an area of memory—usually on the stack—to hold your data, which is sized to fit your data's type.

2. Writes the value 1 to the new area of memory.

3. Updates its list of "variable bindings" for the current scope to indicate that polarity refers to this area of memory.

The compiler does *not* store the name polarity—naming variables is a convenience for you, the programmer. It's a lot easier to remember a name than a memory address. (Debug information stores the name and association; that's how your debugger can show you variable information.)

The compiler performs these steps with every variable assignment. If you call let polarity = 2; let polarity = 2; within the same scope, the first variable remains in existence, but its variable binding is replaced and you have no way to access it.

The following diagram illustrates what's happening:

The code takes advantage of *scope* rules. polarity is bound to a new name within the *inner scope*. When that scope terminates, the original variable binding returns, still attached to the same area of memory. Rebinding variable names—to a new variable—is potentially confusing, which is one reason many development houses ask programmers not to use variable shadowing. Bear in mind these implications with variable shadowing:

- Shadow variables don't replace the name binding until they complete, so you can access the previous version of a variable in the assignment statement.

- Creating a *shadow* variable doesn't affect the original variable. You haven't magically changed it to be mutable; the new variable has its own space in memory. All that changes is that the *name binding* now points to the new value.

- Once you've shadowed a variable, you *can't* access the original variable until the new binding leaves scope.

- Shadowed variables don't have to retain the same type or mutability requirements as the previous variable. In fact, they don't *have* to be related at all because it's an entirely new variable.

- The initial—but unavailable—variable is still occupying memory. If you're concerned about RAM usage, shadowing won't help. The Rust compiler will often remove the unused variable for you, but it's better to be certain that it has been removed.

Sometimes shadowing can help improve the clarity of your code.

When Is Shadowing Useful?

Shadowing is permitted because it can make your code easier to read. The most common argument in favor of permitting shadowing is single-letter variables that get reused in a function. It's not uncommon to encounter code similar to the following:

```
let x = a+b;
// Do something with x
let x = c/d;
// Do something with x
```

For one-shot programs, reusing variable names can be useful; however, if you have to maintain the program for a long time, short variable names aren't the best design choice. Consider the following scenarios:

- If you return to your code in the future, or you're working with other developers, there's very little clue as to what x, a, and other single-letter variable names might mean. Granted, longer variable names means more typing, but with meaningful variable names, you can make your code a lot easier to manage.

- If your function is performing two distinct actions, maybe each action should be a separate function. Each function will have its own scope, so you can use variables without the need to shadow their names.

- If you really don't want to use separate functions, consider restricting the use of short-lived variables to a scope. Scoping your code makes it a lot more obvious to someone reading the code that x doesn't need to live beyond the scope that defines it.

Another use for shadowing is conversion of generic inputs into a concrete type and reusing the name for clarity. Shadowing a type conversion can improve readability. Have a look at this example:

```
fn examine_a_string<S: ToString>(my_string: S) -> String {
  let my_string = my_string.to_string();
  // Perform lots of complicated processing here
  my_string
}
```

The function, examine_a_string(), accepts any type that can be converted into a String with the to_string() function. Forcing the conversion at the top of the function allows you to use the easy-to-read name my_string throughout the function—potentially avoiding confusion. You no longer have named access to the original my_string, and you don't have to worry about what concrete type matched the ToString generic requirement—my_string is guaranteed to have been converted to a String.

Another useful case for variable shadowing is providing *internal* mutability without requiring mutability in your function signature. Look at this example:

```
fn my_complex_function(base: f32, data: &[f32]) -> f32 {
  let mut base = if (base < 0.0) { base + 100.0 } else { base };
  // Iteratively calculate base. You'd probably do something more useful
  // here.
  data.iter().for_each(|n| base += data);
  base
}
```

my_complex_function creates a mutable *shadow* of base and uses it for internal calculation. Many programmers find this easier to read than making the function signature declare mut base: f32 (which does the same thing), and the shadowed variable is neatly contained within the function's scope, so there's limited room for confusion. This pattern is especially common when working with a local clone of a variable; let n = n.clone() is often more readable than let n_clone = n.clone().

When Shouldn't I Use Variable Shadowing?

Rust's variable shadowing rules are controversial and have led to some heated discussions online. Many Rust development houses and experienced developers will instruct you not to use variable shadowing at all. If your code starts to look overly complicated because of shadowing, don't use it. It only takes a moment to type a new variable name, and you will thank yourself when you return to debug your code months later and can't remember why you used a cool shadowing trick.

Detecting Shadowing with Clippy

If you're used to C or C++, you'd expect a compiler warning when you shadow a variable name. Rust specifically permits shadowing, so by default no warning is generated. Clippy can help.

- The optional shadow_same rule can detect when you rebind a variable to itself, for example, let mut x = &mut x.

- Another optional rule named shadow_reuse will warn you about most of the shadowing patterns mentioned in this teaser. It finds cases where you've reused a variable in a shadowed variable. If you prefer to largely prohibit shadowing, shadow_reuse is the rule for you. The teaser code triggers this warning.

- Another optional rule, shadow_unrelated, will warn you when you shadow a variable without ever using the original variable of that name.

If you'd like to enable optional Clippy rules, you may either call Clippy with cargo clippy -- -W clippy:rule_name or add [warn(clippy::rule_name)] statements to your code. Macros have scope: adding the macro to the top of a file in a module applies to to that module only. You can enable the warning crate-wide by prefixing it with an exclamation point: #![warn(clippy:rule_name)].

Further Reading

Scope and Shadowing (Rust by Example)
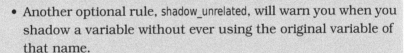
    https://doc.rust-lang.org/rust-by-example/variable_bindings/scope.html

Structure Sizing

structure_sizing/src/main.rs

```rust
use std::mem::size_of;

struct VeryImportantMessage {
    _message_type: u8,
    _destination: u16
}

fn main() {
    println!(
        "VeryImportantMessage occupies {} bytes.",
        size_of::<VeryImportantMessage>()
    );
}
```

Guess the Output

 Try to guess what the output is before moving to the next page.

The program will display the following output:

```
VeryImportantMessage occupies 4 bytes.
```

Discussion

_message_type and _destination are sized as you would expect, occupying 1 and 2 bytes of memory, respectively. So, why does VeryImportantMessage occupy 4 bytes of memory?

By default, Rust makes two promises about the in-memory representation of your structures:

- Structures may be sized differently than their contents for performance reasons.

- Structures may store data in a different order internally than you specified if the optimizer believes it will aid performance.

Most modern CPUs align data on 32-bit boundaries in memory and cache. Accessing 8 bits (one byte) or 16 bits (two bytes) is fast because the CPU provides primitives to do so, and the structures can be packed along 32-bit boundaries.

A 24-bit (3 byte) structure doesn't naturally align to a 32-bit memory map, so by default, Rust wastes 8 bits of memory per struct to ensure fast access to the structure in your computer's memory. This behavior is especially helpful when you're dealing with arrays or other contiguous blocks of 3-byte structures because every other structure would start at the 24th bit of a 32-bit block, reducing cache and read efficiency.

Sometimes this behavior can cause problems, though. For example:

- If you're storing a very large number of 24-bit structures, wasting a byte per structure might exceed your memory allocation—especially on embedded systems.

- If you're interoperating with another language, that language may expect your structures to be *exactly* 24 bits in size. Conversely, a server written in Rust may add padding to structures—surprising the client with padding bytes.

- Likewise, if you're interoperating with other languages, letting Rust rearrange your data in memory can cause bizarre problems when passing data to and from the other language.

Constraining Rust's Optimizer

You can turn off both of Rust's structure optimizations using a decoration named #[repr()], which gives you control over how a struct is represented in memory:

- #[repr(C)] declares that you require interoperability with the C language. Rust won't rearrange the content of your structure.

- #[repr(packed)] tells Rust not to waste space on your structure. This can carry a small performance penalty but guarantees that structures are exactly the right size.

You can combine these decorations. For example, a structure decorated with #[repr(C, packed)] won't rearrange or pad your structure:

```
#[repr(C, packed)]
struct ReallyThreeBytes {
    a: u8,
    b: u16
}
fn main() {
    println!(
      "ReallyThreeBytes occupies {} bytes.",
      size_of::<ReallyThreeBytes>()
    );
}
```

This code prints:

```
ReallyThreeBytes occupies 3 bytes.
```

Further Reading

repr(Rust)
    https://doc.rust-lang.org/nomicon/repr-rust.html

Type Layout
    https://doc.rust-lang.org/reference/type-layout.html

Layout of structs and tuples
    https://rust-lang.github.io/unsafe-code-guidelines/layout/structs-and-tuples.html

To Infinity

linked_list/src/main.rs
```rust
use std::cell::RefCell;
use std::rc::Rc;

type Link = Option<Rc<RefCell<Node>>>;

#[derive(Debug)]
struct Node {
    elem: i32,
    next: Link,
}

fn main() {
    let mut head = Some(Rc::new(
        RefCell::new(Node{ elem: 1, next: None })
    ));
    head
        .as_mut()
        .unwrap()
        .borrow_mut()
        .next = Some(Rc::new(RefCell::new(
            Node{ elem: 2, next: head.clone() })
        ));

    println!("{:?}", head);
}
```

Guess the Output

Try to guess what the output is before moving to the next page.

The program will display node 1, node 2, and then node 1 again. The output repeats itself until the program exits with the following message: thread 'main' has overflowed its stack.

Discussion

Linked lists are one of the first dynamic data structures people encounter in computer science classes and are conceptually simple: each entry in the list contains a pointer to the next entry.[19] Linked lists allow you to easily insert items into the middle of the list—you find your insertion point and copy its next pointer to the new element. Change the previous entry's next to your new entry, and you have inserted into the middle of your list without rearranging existing nodes. You can iterate a linked list by following each node's pointer to the next item. You can visualize a linked list as follows:

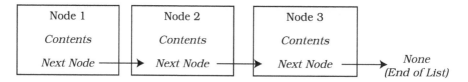

The Next field in each node is an Option that contains either the next node or, in cases where you've reached the end of the list, None.

Implementing Linked Lists in Rust

Although Rust's memory model makes it difficult to create linked lists,[20] you can work around these difficulties by using Rc and RefCell—two low-level structures that are designed to add flexibility to the borrow-checker. Here's what they do:

- Rc provides *reference counting*. When you call get to access an Rc, the reference count is increased by 1. Likewise, when you drop the reference, the count is decreased by 1. When an Rc no longer has references, the contents are deleted. With Rc, you can safely reference the contained structure from other structures and guarantee that the contents get deleted when you're done with them.[21]

19. https://en.wikipedia.org/wiki/Linked_list
20. https://rust-unofficial.github.io/too-many-lists/
21. https://doc.rust-lang.org/std/rc/struct.Rc.html

- RefCell provides a mutable memory location and makes borrow-checking dynamic rather than static. When you borrow the contents of a RefCell, Rust notes that the borrow has occurred at runtime rather than compile time. Although a second mutable borrow can still fail, it will do so as a runtime error rather than a compile-time error.[22]

What Is Reference Counting?

If you've used C# or Java, you may be familiar with reference counting. Reference counting is a form of "garbage collection"—it cleans up unused memory for you, removing the need for you to manage memory yourself. Reference counting works by having an object keep a count of variables that "point" or "refer" to it. Once the reference count hits zero, nothing is using the variable—so it may be safely deleted.

When used together, Rc and RefCell create a dynamic garbage collection structure, much like Java or C#. With this "power couple," you can access individual nodes while remaining confident that your nodes are getting deleted when they're no longer needed (referenced). In addition, by implementing your own garbage collector with Rc and RefCell, you can work around the safety concerns that Rust's borrow-checker has with linked lists.

Rc and RefCell are also handy when you need to make potentially cyclic data structures, which can quickly overwhelm Rust's guaranteed safety checks. In this case, rather than borrowing the entire list when accessing a node, you can dynamically borrow each element as needed. And, with reference counting, you ensure the eventual destruction of unused nodes.

Cyclic References

The example crashes because it creates a *cyclic reference* where the first node's next element points back to the first node, causing the list iteration to continue forever. You can visualize this reference cycle as follows:

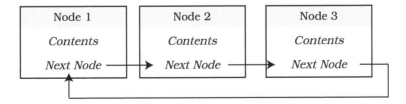

---

22. https://doc.rust-lang.org/std/cell/struct.RefCell.html

Rust cannot delete this structure from memory because the nodes retain references to one another, causing no clear end to the list.

Cyclic references are also a problem with garbage-collected languages. Once a reference cycle is created, there's no way to tell when it's safe to delete a node from memory.

In the example, the default Debug implementation attempts to follow the next node and print its content, which, in turn, loops back to the same node, printing it again. Eventually, the program runs out of call-stack space and crashes.

You can avoid this particular crash by defining your own Debug system that *does not* print the next node. Don't forget to remove #[derive(Debug)] from the Node definition:

```
//#[derive(Debug)]
struct Node {
    elem: i32,
    next: Link,
}

use std::fmt;
impl fmt::Debug for Node {
    fn fmt(&self, f: &mut fmt::Formatter<'_>) -> fmt::Result {
        write!(f, "elem: {}", self.elem)
    }
}
```

This updated code doesn't solve the general problem of cyclic references, though—it simply prevents a program crash.

Generally, you should avoid creating circular structures because they're difficult to iterate safely and delete. Instead, use the Rust standard library's std::collections::LinkedList.[23] Rust's linked list handles node creation and linkage for you.

Should I Use a Linked List?

Linked lists haven't aged well. Modern CPU and memory architectures favor contiguous data for performance, and jumping around memory following next pointers can lead to delays while the computer loads the next area of memory.

---

23. https://doc.rust-lang.org/std/collections/struct.LinkedList.html

Linked list usage remains a controversial topic, but testing shows that Vec outperforms LinkedList in almost every benchmark. Even its primary advantage—inserting an item into the middle of the list—is slower than inserting an item into a vector and then sorting your data.[24]

You may have a specific need for a linked list—but if performance is important to your application, be sure to benchmark against a vector.

Further Reading

Learn Rust with Entirely Too Many Linked Lists
> https://rust-unofficial.github.io/too-many-lists/index.html

Reference Counting
> https://en.wikipedia.org/wiki/Reference_counting

---

24. https://github.com/matklad/vec-vs-list

Double or Nothing

double_or_nothing/src/main.rs
```rust
fn double_it(n: i32) -> i32 {
    n * 2
}

fn double_it(n: f32) -> f32 {
    n * 2.0
}

fn main() {
    println!("2 * 4 = {}", double_it(2));
}
```

Guess the Output

Try to guess what the output is before moving to the next page.

The program will fail to compile, and you'll receive the following error message:

```
error[E0428]: the name "double_it" is defined multiple times
```

Discussion

In C++ and similar languages, redefining a function with different parameter types is known as *function overloading.* It's a common idiom, allowing you to provide similar functionality for multiple types without having to come up with a type-specific function name for each option. For example, the following is valid C++ code:

```
float double_it(float n) {
  return n * 2.0;
}
int double_it(int n) {
  return n * 2;
}
```

Function overloading works in C++ and *not* in Rust because of *name mangling.*[25] When a function is compiled, a compiler-specific name for the function is created and used by the linker to connect function calls to actual memory addresses. In C++, mangled names include both the function name and the *types* of the parameter. double_it(float) and double_it(int) are different functions. Rust only mangles on the function name, so even with different parameter lists, you can't have two functions in the same namespace bearing the same name.

Don't worry, Rust provides a means of accomplishing the same thing. Instead of defining functions with multiple sets of parameters, Rust generics allow you to create a *generic* function that accepts multiple parameter types.

Rust Generics

In Rust, you can still make a double_it function that operates on different types. Rather than redefining the function, you have to use *generics.*[26] Generics are an extremely useful tool for creating reusable code that works across types, but it can quickly become very complicated. Here's a double_it function that works with *any* type that supports multiplication and can be copied by value:

---

25. https://en.wikipedia.org/wiki/Name_mangling
26. https://doc.rust-lang.org/rust-by-example/generics.html

double_or_nothing_working/src/main.rs

```
fn double_it<T>(n: T) -> T
where T: std::ops::Mul<Output = T> + From<i32>
{
    n * 2.into()
}

fn main() {
    println!("2+2 = {}", double_it(2));
}
```

❶ T is added as a generic type to the function signature, and the number to double is defined as requiring type T.

❷ Rust generics constrain the types with which a generic function can operate using the where keyword. You can separate requirements with plus symbols.

The first constraint requires that T implement std::ops::Mul, meaning the type must support the addition operator, and the output of the multiplication must be of type T.

You add a second constraint with + From <i32>, requiring that the input type be constructable from an integer. If you didn't require this constraint, * 2 would fail to compile because Rust could not guarantee that the digit 2 could be converted into a type compatible with the function parameter's type.

❸ Within the function body, you've established that the n parameter *must* support multiplication and be compatible with the integer 2. You can perform the multiplication using normal Rust operators.

Rust generics are *very* powerful, but they can also be intimidating at first. Generic Rust functions and types work by combining traits, establishing the minimum standards a type must meet for the function to be applicable. They are worth the time invested in learning to use them, particularly in library code. By accepting generic types, your code becomes easier for the end user to use. The user's code no longer requires as my_type or into() conversions—it just works. The best part: your generic code retains all of Rust's safety guarantees, explicitly checked for the type the end user decided to use. The cost: generic functions take longer to compile. This is often a price worth paying, but if compilation times become too slow, consider easing up on the generics.

Rust/C++ Interoperability

When you're interoperating with C++, you may miss function name overloading. If you're declaring functions on the Rust side, declare a new function for each parameter type—for example, fn new(name: &str) and fn new_with_age(name: &str, age: u16).[27]

Consuming a C++ library that requires function name overloading is more difficult. Rust won't let you define multiple instances of a function with a single name, making a one-to-one mapping with libraries that rely on function name overloading difficult. You may need to create a "shim" library to map overloaded functions to different function names for Rust to be able to call into your library.

Further Reading

Generics (Rust by Example)

https://doc.rust-lang.org/rust-by-example/generics.html

Rust Generics

https://doc.rust-lang.org/book/ch10-01-syntax.html

Learn Rust—Generics

https://learning-rust.github.io/docs/b4.generics.html

The Rust Programming Language—Generics

http://web.mit.edu/rust-lang_v1.25/arch/amd64_ubuntu1404/share/doc/rust/html/book/first-edition/generics.html

---

27. https://locka99.gitbooks.io/a-guide-to-porting-c-to-rust/content/features_of_rust/polymorphism.html

How Long Is a Vector?

vec_size/src/main.rs

```
fn main() {
    let mut my_vec = Vec::with_capacity(1);
    my_vec.push("Hello");
    println!("{}", my_vec.capacity());
    my_vec.push("World");
    println!("{}", my_vec.capacity());
}
```

Guess the Output

Try to guess what the output is before moving to the next page.

The program will display the following output:

```
1
4
```

Discussion

Vectors contain two things: a length indicating how many elements (items) are stored within the vector and a buffer of contiguous heap memory that contains the data for each of the items, one after the other. This buffer is often larger than the total number of elements stored within the vector.

Vectors are a lot like arrays, but they have a variable size. You can create a vector with a capacity of 0 using new, or you can create a vector with a user-specified capacity size using with_capacity. The *capacity* represents the total size of the vector.

When you add an item to a vector, the vector checks to see if the vector's length—number of actual items in the vector—is less than the vector's capacity. If it is, then adding to the vector is straightforward: the vector's length is incremented, and the item is moved to the next available space in the vector. If there isn't free space at the end of the buffer, the vector:

1. Allocates a new buffer with enough space for twice the new vector's length.
2. Moves the existing buffer to the beginning of the new buffer.
3. Releases the old buffer.
4. Increments length and adds the new item to the end of the new, larger, buffer.

You can visualize a vector's growth as follows:

Vector growth seems like a lot of work, but it comes with very real performance benefits. The entire vector is guaranteed to be adjacent in your computer's memory, making it very cache-friendly—operating on vectors is *very* fast. Like all benefits, it comes with a trade-off: when you exceed the vector's capacity, extending the vector is a much slower operation.

Vec includes a constructor named with_capacity that lets you specify the exact size (in elements) of the new vector. If you never exceed this size, the vector will never reallocate memory.

In the example, calling Vec::with_capacity(1) creates a new vector with enough capacity for one element. It then adds a new entry ("Hello") to the vector, using that slot, and filling the vector. At this point, the vector has no idea if it'll ever need to increase its capacity again, so it stays at 1. The code then pushes another new entry ("World") into the vector; this time, however, there's no room, so the vector adds three more spaces to allow for future growth, leading to a capacity of 4.

Rust's vector growth strategy isn't guaranteed in the language standard and may change. At the time of this writing, Rust uses a "growth factor" of 2. In most cases, the vector will double in size when it needs additional capacity. If you are sequentially adding many items to a vector, this operation can cause a lot of memory reallocation, potentially causing performance problems.

Vector Tips

When working with vectors, keep a few things in mind:

- If you have a rough idea of how much data you *might* need to store, use Vec::with_capacity to reserve an appropriate amount of space ahead of time—doing so avoids memory reallocations altogether.

- If you're adding lots of data, try using Vec::extend so that Rust can see the size of the data you're adding and reallocate only once. extend only avoids allocation when collecting data from a source with a known length. Copying from one vector to another allows Rust to allocate exactly the space it needs for the new vector because the length is known. Likewise, any iterator that implements ExactSizeIterator benefits from this optimization.[28] An arbitrarily sized iterator may repeatedly allocate because the size of the data you're copying isn't known ahead of time.

---

28. https://doc.rust-lang.org/std/iter/trait.ExactSizeIterator.html

- Add elements to the end of your vectors using push rather than at a specific slot using insert. Although insert gives you more control, it's a lot slower than push because Rust needs to rearrange the vector to make room for your new element. If you *need* to insert an element at the front, the VecDeque structure is a better choice.[29]

Further Reading

std::vec::Vec

> https://doc.rust-lang.org/std/vec/struct.Vec.html

---

29. https://doc.rust-lang.org/std/collections/struct.VecDeque.html

Mutable Immutables

mutable_immutable/src/main.rs
```rust
fn main() {
    let life_the_universe = &mut 41;
    *life_the_universe += 1;
    println!("Life, the Universe and Everything: {}", life_the_universe);
}
```

Guess the Output

 Try to guess what the output is before moving to the next page.

The program will display the following output:

```
Life, the Universe and Everything: 42
```

Discussion

The surprising part of this teaser is that the life_the_universe variable is immutable, yet you're able to change its contents. To understand how this is possible, look at the following illustration:

```
let life_the_universe = &mut 41;
```

Create an immutable variable named life_the_universe.

The area of memory exists in temporary (scope lifetime) memory, and contains the number 41.

life_the_universe contains a mutable reference to an area of memory.

Notice a few tricks in play here:

- You can declare a reference to a *literal*.[30] When you do, Rust creates a temporary area of memory containing the desired value, and because the literal is mutable, you can change it.[31]

- The life_the_universe reference itself remains immutable—once you define the reference, it forever points to the same area of memory, and you can't change it.

- You can de-reference your immutable reference using the * operator, which gives you mutable access to its contents.

The following code works on variables, as well, and is a little clearer:

```
let mut life = 40;
let the_universe = &mut life;
*the_universe += 2;
println!("{}", the_universe);
```

Making life a mutable variable clearly marks life as a variable that expects changes. So when you take a mutable reference to life (the_universe), you expect

---

30. https://doc.rust-lang.org/reference/expressions/literal-expr.html
31. https://doc.rust-lang.org/reference/expressions.html#temporary-lifetimes

to be able to change its contents. The mutability and borrow-checking rules enforced by the Rust compiler are still obeyed:

- life is mutable and may change.
- the_universe is immutable because it will always point at life once it's been set.
- De-referencing the_universe allows you to change the contents of life.
- Rust's borrow-checking rules still apply to mutable references. You can't mutably borrow the memory area pointed to by life more than once, can't reference it once it has left the active scope, and can't mutably share it between threads without synchronization primitives.

You can arrange your code either way—but making life's mutability obvious makes it easier to read. Rust's mutability rules don't mind which way you lay out the code; it works the same either way. The pattern of a mutable variable—a label for an area of memory—accessed by other variables is a common one.

Borrowed Mutability

It's rare that you'll need to borrow a literal in this fashion. Most of the time, it's much clearer to create a variable of the native type as mutable and work on it directly. The mutability is less confusing, and your code is potentially faster when the compiler doesn't optimize (by removing) de-references. You generally won't need to directly declare the *contents* of a variable as a mutable reference.

Mutably borrowed variables are very useful. You can pass x: &mut my_type into functions, and the function can change the original (borrowed) value rather than having to return an all-new structure. You're still benefitting from the immutability of the x variable because x is a pointer to an area in memory, which means you can't inadvertently change the pointer itself or the memory location to which the reference points. You can, however, change the data to which the reference points because the *borrow* remains mutable.

In embedded systems and driver code, it's common to encounter pointers and references to mutable memory. Rust code can act just like C code in this respect but with added protection against mutating state by mistake.[32]

Further Reading

References and Borrowing
> https://doc.rust-lang.org/book/ch04-02-references-and-borrowing.html

Mutability (Rust by Example)
> https://doc.rust-lang.org/rust-by-example/scope/borrow/mut.html

---

32. https://docs.rust-embedded.org/book/peripherals/a-first-attempt.html

Sleepless in Tokio

sleepless/Cargo.toml

```
[package]
name = "sleepless"
version = "0.1.0"
edition = "2018"

[dependencies]
tokio = { version = "1.7", features = ["full"] }
```

sleepless/src/main.rs

```
use tokio::join;
use std::time::Duration;

async fn count_and_wait(n: u64) -> u64 {
    println!("Starting {}", n);
    std::thread::sleep(Duration::from_millis(n * 100));
    println!("Returning {}", n);
    n
}

#[tokio::main]
async fn main() -> Result<(), Box<dyn std::error::Error>> {
    // Join runs multiple tasks concurrently and returns when they all
    // complete execution.
    join!(count_and_wait(1), count_and_wait(2), count_and_wait(3));
    Ok(())
}
```

Guess the Output

 Try to guess what the output is before moving to the next page.

The program will display the following output:

```
Starting 1
Returning 1
Starting 2
Returning 2
Starting 3
Returning 3
```

Discussion

The outcome is surprising because the join macro promises to run the three instances of count_and_wait concurrently, but the output shows that the tasks are running sequentially, which tends to surprise newcomers to Rust's async system. Understanding the differences between asynchronous and thread programming can help you avoid pitfalls—and help you pick the right model for your program.

Asynchronous programs and multithreaded programs operate differently, each with their own strengths and weaknesses. Asynchronous (Future-based) tasks aren't the same as threaded tasks, and they require some care to ensure that they operate concurrently. However, it's entirely possible to run an asynchronous program on one thread.

The diagram on page 83 shows the basic differences between threaded and asynchronous execution:

In a *threaded* model, each task operates inside a full operating system-supported thread. Threads are scheduled independently of other threads and processes. An *asynchronous* model stores tasks in a task queue and runs them until they *yield* control back to the executing program.

Let's examine a few approaches to running this teaser concurrently.

Native Threads

Threads are *preemptively* scheduled by your operating system. While the thread is suspended, other threads continue to run. A purely threaded version of this teaser looks like this:

async_threaded/src/main.rs
```rust
use std::thread;
use std::time::Duration;
```

Threaded Execution:

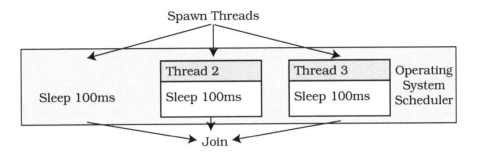

Asynchronous Execution:

Spawn Tasks

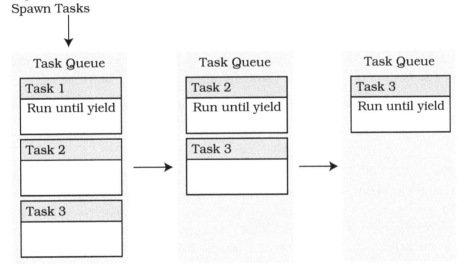

```
fn count_and_wait(n: u64) -> u64 {
    println!("Starting {}", n);
    std::thread::sleep(Duration::from_millis(n * 100));
    println!("Returning {}", n);
    n
}

fn main() -> Result<(), Box<dyn std::error::Error>> {
    let a = thread::spawn(|| count_and_wait(1));
    let b = thread::spawn(|| count_and_wait(2));
    let c = thread::spawn(|| count_and_wait(3));
    a.join().unwrap();
    b.join().unwrap();
    c.join().unwrap();
    Ok(())
}
```

The program spawns three threads, and they each run concurrently. Because the program calls sleep and delays execution on each thread, you're almost—subject to having a *really* busy computer—sure to see the following output:

```
Starting 1
Starting 2
Starting 3
Returning 1
Returning 2
Returning 3
```

Threads provide excellent concurrency, but it comes at a cost. Threads have their own context maintained by the operating system. Starting a thread requires a system call, which can be slow if you need to make *many* threads. Different operating systems have varying limitations, but there's a hard limit to the number of threads you can create—and your OS is generally not designed to schedule thousands of threads at a time. Native thread syntax can also be clunkier than an equivalent async join or await call.

Threads start running as soon as you call Thread::spawn. The thread then runs—scheduled by the operating system—until it's done or sent a termination signal.

Asynchronous Tasks

Asynchronous tasks are *cooperatively scheduled*. The operating system doesn't intervene to ensure that each thread gets a fair allocation of execution time. Tasks run until they yield control. Yielding returns control to the executor—the code responsible for maintaining the async environment. Tasks yield when:

- The task returns a result (either an error message or a value).
- The task completes execution.
- The task awaits one or more tasks.
- The task explicitly calls yield_now(), suspending itself until the executor resumes it.

Used correctly, asynchronous task-based code can provide fantastic performance. This is especially true for I/O bound programs—programs that have to wait for databases, files on disk, or other processes to complete. Lightweight tasks send requests to the other systems and await a result. Each task queue can then keep processing requests *very* fast, executing tasks only when the requested data is ready for them.

What Is an Executor?

Rust's async implementation provides everything you need to make an asynchronous environment, but it only provides the functionality required to implement an executor. The executor is responsible for tracking spawned tasks, executing them, and providing services such as yield.

Tokio is one of the most popular executors, providing a "batteries-included" system with functionality available for most common tasks. The std-async and futures crates are also popular. If you need specific functionality, you can also write your own executor.

Many executors allocate tasks to queues in a group of threads, but they don't have to. Most schedule multiple tasks per thread—known as M:N green threading—but an async setup can be entirely single-threaded.

Other platforms use this paradigm as well. NodeJS, Erlang/Elixir, and various .NET systems provide similar functionality.

As it turns out, asynchronous tasks only provide outstanding performance if you play by their rules and avoid any *blocking* calls. Blocking calls suspend process execution and resume when the call is complete. Furthermore, blocking calls don't yield control back to the executor—a call to Thread::sleep suspends the entire thread's execution, *including* the executor. That's why the example program runs serially, even though the join macro promises concurrency.

For the common task of sleeping, Tokio provides a safe, nonblocking call to make a task pause for the specified time. Replace Thread::sleep the count_and_wait function with the following code:

```
tokio::time::sleep(Duration::from_millis(n*100)).await;
```

Run the program, and you'll see the same output as the threaded version, meaning your program ran concurrently.

Asynchronous Blocking Tasks

Sometimes, you *need* to block execution; for example, when you have a long-running task, need to communicate with some hardware that doesn't provide an async friendly code wrapper, or have to use another library. tokio provides a function for these situations that won't stall the execution pipeline:

```
let blocking_task = tokio::spawn_blocking(|| {
  // Do something really slow and blocking here
});

// Run the task
blocking_task.await.unwrap();
```

The spawn_blocking code tells tokio that your task will block, and tokio will spawn it inside its own thread, suspending the current task until the thread returns. Your task runs in the background, and your executor can keep processing other tasks. Notice that the blocking task still awaits a return; Tokio will awaken the parent task when the blocking task completes.

Long-Running Asynchronous Tasks

Occasionally, you need to perform some heavy computation inside your async task. A task may call yield_now at any time to suspend operation and let other tasks run. When the scheduler returns to the task, it'll continue where it left off. For example, have a look at this code:

```
async fn my_big_task() {
  for i in 0..1_000_000 {
    // Do something intensive with i
    tokio::task::yield_now();
  }
}
```

This task will yield control back to the executor after each calculation, which reduces the stalling effects of your heavy calculation without creating a thread.

Choosing Threaded or Asynchronous Operation

tokio and other systems provide an async version of the more common operations that require input/output. Reading and writing files, connections to databases, and even logging are available in executor-friendly formats. Task-based asynchronous code can be amazingly fast for programs that frequently have to wait for another system. Web and other servers often benefit significantly from a task-based structure and provide very high throughput.

Threads are more appropriate for CPU-bound tasks and tasks that *must* block. Threads incur their own overhead, but if the threaded task is sufficiently "heavy" in terms of CPU load, they can outperform asynchronous task-based systems. In the embedded world, or when writing performance-critical code, you often want to favor threads because you can control their scheduling properties (and pin them to individual CPUs)—providing much more of a guarantee of execution time.

Rayon: Task-Based Threading

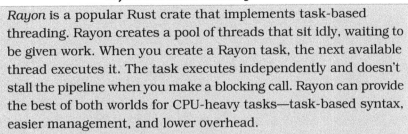 *Rayon* is a popular Rust crate that implements task-based threading. Rayon creates a pool of threads that sit idly, waiting to be given work. When you create a Rayon task, the next available thread executes it. The task executes independently and doesn't stall the pipeline when you make a blocking call. Rayon can provide the best of both worlds for CPU-heavy tasks—task-based syntax, easier management, and lower overhead.

Rayon performs very well but is still frequently outperformed on input/output bound server tasks by a more traditional asynchronous setup. Of course, you can mix the two, but you'll have to pay attention to the size of your worker thread pools to ensure that your executor isn't starved of CPU time.

Further Reading

Asynchronous Programming in Rust
> https://rust-lang.github.io/async-book/01_getting_started/01_chapter.html

Rust Futures
> https://github.com/rust-lang/futures-rs

Tokio
> https://github.com/rayon-rs/rayon

Async-Std
> https://github.com/async-rs/async-std

Rayon
> https://github.com/rayon-rs/rayon

Hello, Bonjour

hello_bonjour/src/main.rs
```rust
fn main() {
    let hello = || println!("Hello World");
    let hello = || println!("Bonjour le monde");
    hello();
}
```

Guess the Output

Try to guess what the output is before moving to the next page.

The program will display the following output:

```
Bonjour le monde
```

Discussion

In Puzzle 16, Double or Nothing, on page 69, you saw that you cannot shadow functions with identical names—even if the parameter list is different. Function shadowing rules don't apply to closures (sometimes known as *lambda functions*).

Closures don't actually *have* names. The variable that holds a closure is a *pointer* to the area of memory containing the function. The variables that point to the closures are subject to the same shadowing rules as other variables (Puzzle 13, Reverse the Polarity of the Neutron Flow, on page 53). Function name mangling doesn't apply, because closures don't have function names to mangle; they're, instead, identified by the variable that points to them.

You may create as many shadow lambda functions as you like, subject to the same scoping rules as variables. Once you've re-declared an identifier to point to a different closure, the original variable remains inaccessible until—or if—the new declaration leaves the active scope.

Shadowing closure definitions in this way isn't particularly useful—it illustrates the fact that closures obey *variable* rather than function shadowing rules.

Rather than creating a closure and immediately replacing it, you probably want to *select* one to run. You can perform this selection at compilation time with *static dispatch*, or at runtime with *dynamic dispatch*.

Static Dispatch

Static dispatch allows your program to make behavioral decisions at compile time. Two major approaches to implementing static dispatch in Rust are conditional compilation and constant functions. Let's start by looking at conditional compilation.

Feature Flags and Conditional Compilation

Rust supports a broad range of conditional compilation systems.[33] You can change how your program compiles on different platforms, on different

---

33. https://doc.rust-lang.org/reference/conditional-compilation.html

compilers, or even in response to your shell's environment variables. Feature flags can be very useful for tweaking how your program interacts with different systems. Rust also provides *feature flags*, allowing you to customize your code to fit the end user's requirements.[34]

Let's test conditional compilation by adding some feature flags to the Cargo.toml file:

hello_bonjour_static/Cargo.toml
```
[package]
name = "hello_bonjour_static"
version = "0.1.0"
edition = "2018"

[features]
english = []
french = []

[dependencies]
```

Next, we modify the code to make each definition of hello conditional upon a feature flag:

hello_bonjour_static/src/main.rs
```
fn main() {
    #[cfg(feature = "english")]
    let hello = || println!("Hello World");
    #[cfg(feature = "french")]
    let hello = || println!("Bonjour le monde");
    hello();
}
```

If you run the program with cargo run, it will fail to compile because no hello function is defined. However, you can run the program with cargo run --features english to be greeted in English or cargo run --features french to be greeted in French.

Constant Functions

If you're working within the ever-growing subset of code that can be executed inside constant functions (with const fn), you can also implement static dispatch using these functions. Here's an example:

hello_bonjour_const/src/main.rs
```
enum Language { English, French }

const fn hello(language: Language) -> &'static str {
    match language {
        Language::English => "Hello World",
        Language::French => "Bonjour le monde",
    }
}
```

---

34. https://doc.rust-lang.org/cargo/reference/features.html

```
fn main() {
    println!("{}", hello(Language::English));
}
```

In this code, hello() is a constant function. It's evaluated entirely at compile time, so the language parameter must come from a constant source.

At the other end of the spectrum, dynamic dispatch makes decisions while your program runs. Let's have a look.

Dynamic Dispatch

Dynamic dispatch is a fancy computer-science phrase for "use a match statement to decide what to do at runtime." The following is an example:

```
enum Language = { English, French };
let language = Language::English;
let hello = match language {
  Language::English => || println!("Hello World"),
  Language::French => || println!("Bonjour le monde"),
};
```

Dynamic dispatch is slower than compile-time decision-making, but not by much. A simple match statement is *very* fast on modern computers—more complicated match statements may be slower, especially when they occur inside a large loop. Notice that the closures still act like a variable: you can return complete closures from a match statement. This is because they *are* variables, of type Fn (for immutable functions) or FnMut (that can mutate captured variables). Runtime selection of closures is *very* powerful when you need to customize your execution flow.

When Should I Use Dynamic vs. Static Dispatch?

Dynamic dispatch is a good place to start, but static dispatch is very useful when:

- You need to keep your program as small as possible, excluding features that won't be used on a given target.

- You want to optionally support additional features. For example, a graphics library may require a wasm feature flag to enable Web Assembly support. Using conditional compilation is necessary when you need to only compile parts of your code when targeting specific environments—WASM-specific functions won't exist when compiling against other targets. Conditional compilation can also let you change your program's behavior when compiled to target a specific operating system.

- You want to implement several algorithms and test which one is best. Static dispatch lets you pick one at compilation time, with no additional cost added to your benchmarks.

Localization

 It's uncommon for larger applications to provide text in multiple languages with different functions. It's far more common to define all the text in your application in "language files" and load the appropriate language specified in your program's configuration file.

Further Reading

Features

https://doc.rust-lang.org/cargo/reference/features.html

Const Functions

https://doc.rust-lang.org/reference/const_eval.html#const-functions

Closures

https://doc.rust-lang.org/book/ch13-01-closures.html

Tying a Gordian Knot

gordian_knot/src/main.rs
```rust
#[derive(Debug)]
struct Parser<'a> {
    body: String,
    subtext : &'a str,
}

fn main() {
    let mut document = Parser {
        body: "Hello".to_string(),
        subtext: ""
    };
    document.subtext = &document.body;

    let b = document;
    println!("{:?}", b);
}
```

Guess the Output

Try to guess what the output is before moving to the next page.

The program will fail to compile with the following message:

```
error[E0505]: cannot move out of `document` because it is borrowed
  --> gordian_knot\src\main.rs:14:13
```

Discussion

It's not surprising that this example fails to compile; setting up references within a structure to other parts of the structure looks like a code smell. What *is* surprising is that the compiler makes it nearly to the end of the code before it flags an error on the second-to-last line.

Structural References

Storing a reference in a struct is entirely valid, but you *must provide* a lifetime annotation for both the struct and the reference. In this example, the structure itself has a lifetime specified: struct Parser<'a>. And the structure's lifetime is tied to the stored reference: subtext : &'a str. The lifetime syntax is illustrated as follows:

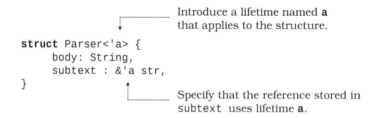

Connecting the struct lifetime to the reference's lifetime helps Rust provide a lifetime guarantee. You cannot instantiate a variable of type Parser unless the reference it contains is certain to remain valid longer than the structure's lifetime. Lifetime annotations help Rust's lifetime checker help you. You can't inadvertently create a reference, destroy the original variable, and then use the Parser variable by mistake; attempting to use an expired reference will generate a compilation error.

But don't be fooled—lifetimes and references in the structure are not the cause of the problem. What about the self-referential assignment? Could *that* be the problem? Let's find out.

Self-Referential Assignment

The example assigns part of a Parser structure to another part of itself:

```
a.subtext = &a.body;
```

Self-referential assignments may look suspicious, but surprisingly, the code is valid, so it compiles. The assignment doesn't violate any of Rust's memory safety rules:

- Storing a reference to itself does not violate the lifetime specifications. A reference to part of the structure *has* to live as long as the structure. No problem there.

- body is borrowed immutably, and only once. No borrow checker rules are violated.

If the borrow checker and lifetimes are also not the problem, then why won't the example compile?

Valid but Unchangeable Structures

Once document is assigned a self-reference, it's in an unusual state: it remains valid but cannot be modified. As a result, the following Rust safety constraints kick in:

- The lifetime a requires that the struct's body member remain valid. Dropping body would invalidate the lifetime guarantee for subtext.

- The borrow checker remembers that subtext is immutably borrowing body. Any attempt to mutate body—including changing or dropping it—will fail.

Oddly enough, Rust lets you create a Gordian knot—a complicated problem that seems too difficult to solve. document is valid, but using it is almost always not. When you assign subtext to be a reference (pointer) to body—a reference within the same structure—you create two safety guarantees:

Assign subtext to body:

```
                            a  Parser {
Lifetime a                         body: "Hello World"
subtext and Parser share the
same lifetime requirement.      a  subtext: pointer            subtext is borrowing body
                               }
```

The innocuous-looking statement let b = a triggers a borrow-checker violation. Assigning document to b triggers a move. The memory storing document is moved into b. This counts as a mutation, and the borrow checker refuses to let you perform the move because document.body is borrowed immutably. The move fails even in a *release mode* build—where the compiler will almost certainly optimize away the actual memory copying/movement. The borrow-checking violation occurs because your Parser is borrowing from itself:

Assigning b to document:

Editing document is also very difficult. If you attempt to edit document.body with document.body = "World".to_string(), the borrow checker flags the edit and prevents you from doing so. You have created a mutable read-only variable.

It's also really difficult to get rid of document. std::mem::drop(document) also fails with a borrow-checker error. Rust's attempts to Drop the structure violate the borrow checker's rules, because the stucture is already borrowed.

So, how do you untie this seemingly impossible knot?

Untying the Gordian Knot

One method of untying the Gordian knot is to place it in its own scope. The following code compiles:

```rust
fn main() {
    {
        let mut a = Parser {
            body: "Hello".to_string(),
            subtext: ""
        };
        a.subtext = &a.body;
    }
}
```

You can safely use self-referential structures inside of functions for this reason. Rust knows that the entire structure is vanishing when it leaves the active scope, and it disposes of it in one fell swoop.

Why Use Self-Referential Structures?

If your structure holds a large amount of data, storing references to part of the stored data can be very useful. For example, a parser might need to store references to parts of the source code it's reading. Here are a few suggestions to help you when you need to do this:

- Consider extracting self-referential systems into separate structures that refer to the parent variable. This solution makes deletion of the objects explicit: you can safely drop the child object at any time, but Rust's lifetime protection still guarantees that the parent object must outlive its children.

- Limit the use of self-referencing objects to short-lived scopes that can be safely deleted.

- If you're referencing index data, you could store the index to which you are referring rather than a direct reference/pointer to the referenced data.

- If all else fails, use reference counting (Rc) and weak pointers to untangle your data.[35]

Rust's borrow-checking and lifetime checking features can sometimes add a little complexity to your code. It's a trade-off: on one hand, it's very difficult to create dangerous code. On the other, sometimes you'd like to perform a safe operation but have to jump through a few extra hoops to *prove* that your operation is safe to Rust.

Further Reading

Validating References with Lifetimes
   https://doc.rust-lang.org/book/ch10-03-lifetime-syntax.html

References and Borrowing
   http://web.mit.edu/rust-lang_v1.25/arch/amd64_ubuntu1404/share/doc/rust/html/book/first-edition/references-and-borrowing.html

---

35. https://doc.rust-lang.org/std/rc/struct.Weak.html

Waiting for Godot

waiting_for_godot/Cargo.toml
```toml
[package]
name = "waiting_for_godot"
version = "0.1.0"
edition = "2018"

[dependencies]
tokio = { version = "1", features = ["full"] }
```

waiting_for_godot/src/main.rs
```rust
async fn hello() {
    println!("Hello, World!")
}

#[tokio::main]
pub async fn main() -> Result<(), Box<dyn std::error::Error>> {
    hello();
    Ok(())
}
```

Guess the Output

Try to guess what the output is before moving to the next page.

The program will not print anything.

Discussion

You explored asynchronous task scheduling in Puzzle 19, Sleepless in Tokio , on page 81, where you learned that tasks are executed by your program's Executor, running until they yield control back to the task queue. Tasks only yield when they return a value or error, call another asynchronous task, finish execution, or call yield_now. Tasks also don't *start* when you call them. When you call a function decorated with the async keyword, it returns a *Future*.[36] Calling an async-decorated function doesn't *execute* the function—instead, it packages it up for future execution.

Let's take a look at the life cycle of an asynchronous function:

1. Create an asynchronous function, using the async keyword.
```
async fn my_function() { ... }
```

2. Executing the function creates a Future, wrapping your function in a promise of future execution.
```
let promise = my_function()  ──→  Returns a Future<my_function>
                                  my_function does not execute yet!
```

3. Add the Future<my_function> to the Executor's task queue:
```
You may use any    my_function().await
of these methods   spawn(promise)
                   join!(promise, -other futures-)
                   select!(promise, -other futures-)
```

Executing an async function is a two-step process. The first creates a *promise* of future execution. Separating these steps gives you the flexibility to decide how you want to actually run your function.

Asynchronous Future Choices

When you call a function decorated with the async keyword, the function doesn't automatically start. Instead, it returns a variable implementing the Future trait.[37] Futures are the primary building block of asynchronous programming. When you create a Future, you're indicating that your task is packaged up and ready to go. Once you have a Future, you may:

- Call spawn to add the task to your executor's task queue and not wait around for an answer.

---

36. https://doc.rust-lang.org/std/future/index.html
37. https://doc.rust-lang.org/std/future/trait.Future.html

- await a result from the task, yielding control to other tasks until a result is available.

- Use join macros to execute several tasks at once and wait for all of them to complete.

- Call select to execute several tasks and continue when one of them returns a result.

Let's use await to execute the hello() function.

Executing Hello

You can make the program print Hello, World! by telling the main function to await a result from hello(). To do so, you'd adjust your code as follows:

```
#[tokio::main]
pub async fn main() -> Result<(), Box<dyn std::error::Error>> {
  hello().await;
  Ok(())
}
```

The await instructs the tokio executor to suspend task execution and commence execution of hello. When the hello() function finishes executing, the function yields control to the main function—which then exits. With this modification, the program will operate as you probably expect, displaying the following output:

```
Hello, World!
```

Future Enhancements to Clippy

Creating a Future but not executing it (via spawning the task or using the await keyword) is a very common error for developers new to Rust asynchronous programming. The Rust compiler emits a warning that your function will not execute unless you await or spawn it.

Further Reading

Asynchronous Programming in Rust
> https://rust-lang.github.io/async-book/

Rust Futures
> https://doc.rust-lang.org/std/future/trait.Future.html

Demystifying Closures, Futures and async-await in Rust-Part 3: Async & Await
> https://medium.com/@alistairisrael/demystifying-closures-futures-and-async-await-in-rust-part-3-async-await-9ed20eede7a4

Constant Loops

const_loop/src/main.rs
```rust
const fn fib(n: u128) -> u128 {
    let mut a = 1;
    let mut b = 1;
    for _ in 2..n {
        let tmp = a + b;
        a = b;
        b = tmp;
    }
    b
}

fn main() {
    for i in 0..5 {
        println!("Fib {} = {}", i, fib(i));
    }
}
```

Guess the Output

Try to guess what the output is before moving to the next page.

The program will fail to compile with the following error message:

```
'for' is not allowed in a 'const fn'
```

Discussion

Marking a function as const causes the function to run at *compile time* rather than at runtime. When a function runs at compile time, the compiler calculates the results beforehand from constant inputs, which can help speed up complex calculations that you might need later.

Suppose your program requires a *lot* of Fibonacci numbers. Without a const function, your program would need to recalculate the numbers as needed, and possibly more than once. However, by using a const function, you can store these numbers as constant values in your program, dramatically improving your program's performance.

const functions—a relatively new Rust feature—are gradually becoming more powerful. However, at the time of this publication, you cannot use the following Rust features inside of a constant function:[38]

- Floating-point operations (you can move them around, but you can't work with them).

- Dynamic trait types.

- Generic bounds on parameters other than Sized.

- Raw pointer operations.

- Union (enum) field access.

- transmute and similar memory operations.

As it turns out, for loops fall into the unavailable category because they require a Range—prohibited because of the generic bounds restriction. This makes the example code fail to compile.

Other loop types work fine, though. For example, you can rewrite the example using a while loop:

---

38. https://doc.rust-lang.org/reference/const_eval.html#const-functions

const_loop_works/src/main.rs
```rust
const fn fib(n: u128) -> u128 {
    let mut a = 1;
    let mut b = 1;
    let mut counter = 2;
    while counter < n {
        let tmp = a + b;
        a = b;
        b = tmp;
        counter += 1;
    }
    b
}

fn main() {
    for i in 0..5 {
        println!("Fib {} = {}", i, fib(i));
    }
}
```

Rust is adding more and more const fn support over time, as the compile-time environment is extended to support it.

Constant Guarantees

C++ includes a facility to label a function as constexpr. In C++, this doesn't guarantee that the function runs at compile-time—it suggests it. Rust is more strict: constant functions must run at compile time and not during regular program execution. This ensures that you know exactly what resources you are utilizing by executing the function: nothing at runtime, at the expense of longer compilation times.[39]

C++ constexpr launched with a very restrictive set of supported features, and added to the available functionality over time. Rust is following a similar trajectory.

Using Constant Functions

As you just learned, constant functions can shift some of the calculation burden to compile time, helping to speed up your program's execution. Here are a few scenarios in which constant functions are useful:

- Programs often rely on the results of complex calculations with limited sets of input. With const variables and functions, you can build lookup

---

39. https://en.cppreference.com/w/cpp/language/constexpr

tables of the required results, skipping the need to perform these calculations at runtime.

• Sometimes your program relies on a predetermined piece of math, yet showing the work can help explain what your program does. Moving that work to compile time removes the runtime performance penalty for performing the calculation—and you're still free to tweak the math in the source code.

Note, however, that constant functions have some serious limitations on the types of data they can use. An alternative is to write a separate program to calculate a lookup table and then copy and paste the results into a const variable.

Further Reading

Const Functions
> https://doc.rust-lang.org/reference/const_eval.html#const-functions

Home on the Range

```rust
fn main() {
    .. .. ..;
}
```

Guess the Output

Try to guess what the output is before moving to the next page.

The program will compile and run, but it won't display any output.

Discussion

The .. symbol has a few meanings in Rust:

- .. without numbers indicates a range containing every available value.

- 1..3 creates a range that starts at 1 and stops at 2.

- 1.. creates a range that starts at 1 and continues forever.

- ..10 creates a range that includes every number up to but not including 10.

- Used on an indexed type, [..] creates a RangeFull value.

- In a match or if let statement, MyOption(field, ..) ignores all other parameters that you haven't explicitly named.

The example is accumulating range expressions. No ranges are provided, but the syntax remains technically valid. The example compiles, but it is very unlikely that you will ever need it.

Rust was developed in the open and has accumulated a surprising number of expressions that compile but aren't useful. The Rust language repository contains a collection of these oddities.[40] The repo even includes an example that takes this example to an extreme length:

```
fn punch_card() -> impl std::fmt::Debug {
    ..=..=..  ..        ..  ..  ..  ..      ..  ..  ..  ..      ..  ..=..  ..
    ..=..  ..=..        ..  ..  ..  ..      ..  ..  ..  ..      ..=..=..=..
    ..=..  ..=..        ..=..  ..=..        ..  ..=..=..        ..  ..=..  ..
    ..=..=..  ..        ..=..  ..=..        ..=..  ..  ..       ..  ..=..  ..
    ..=..  ..=..        ..=..  ..=..        ..  ..=..  ..       ..  ..=..  ..
    ..=..  ..=..        ..=..  ..=..        ..  ..  ..=..       ..  ..=..  ..
    ..=..  ..=..        ..  ..=..=..        ..=..=..  ..        ..  ..=..  ..
}
```

Every language has accumulated a similar list of not so helpful—yet entertaining—syntax that surprises you by compiling. Finding them can be fun.

---

40. https://github.com/rust-lang/rust/blob/master/src/test/ui/weird-exprs.rs

Placeholders

When I found out that you could use .. as a function body, I was very tempted to use it to indicate placeholders—code that still needed to be written. Rust has a built-in solution: the todo! macro.[41]

Further Reading

Rust Weird Expressions

https://github.com/rust-lang/rust/blob/master/src/test/ui/weird-exprs.rs

---

41. https://doc.rust-lang.org/std/macro.todo.html

Bibliography

[KN19]   Steve Klabnik and Carol Nichols. *The Rust Programming Language (Covers Rust 2018)*. No Starch Press, San Francisco, CA, 2019. Steve Klabnik and Carol Nichols. *The Rust Programming Language (Covers Rust 2018)*. No Starch Press, San Francisco, CA, 2019.

[Wol21] Herbert Wolverson. *Hands-on Rust*. The Pragmatic Bookshelf, Raleigh, NC, 2021.

Index

Thank you!

We hope you enjoyed this book and that you're already thinking about what you want to learn next. To help make that decision easier, we're offering you this gift.

Head on over to https://pragprog.com right now, and use the coupon code BUYANOTHER2022 to save 30% on your next ebook. Offer is void where prohibited or restricted. This offer does not apply to any edition of the *The Pragmatic Programmer* ebook.

And if you'd like to share your own expertise with the world, why not propose a writing idea to us? After all, many of our best authors started off as our readers, just like you. With a 50% royalty, world-class editorial services, and a name you trust, there's nothing to lose. Visit https://pragprog.com/become-an-author/ today to learn more and to get started.

We thank you for your continued support, and we hope to hear from you again soon!

The Pragmatic Bookshelf

Pragmatic Bookshelf

SAVE 30%!
Use coupon code
BUYANOTHER2022

Hands-on Rust

Rust is an exciting new programming language combining the power of C with memory safety, fearless concurrency, and productivity boosters—and what better way to learn than by making games. Each chapter in this book presents hands-on, practical projects ranging from "Hello, World" to building a full dungeon crawler game. With this book, you'll learn game development skills applicable to other engines, including Unity and Unreal.

Herbert Wolverson
(342 pages) ISBN: 9781680508161. $47.95
https://pragprog.com/book/hwrust

Programming WebAssembly with Rust

WebAssembly fulfills the long-awaited promise of web technologies: fast code, type-safe at compile time, execution in the browser, on embedded devices, or anywhere else. Rust delivers the power of C in a language that strictly enforces type safety. Combine both languages and you can write for the web like never before! Learn how to integrate with JavaScript, run code on platforms other than the browser, and take a step into IoT. Discover the easy way to build cross-platform applications without sacrificing power, and change the way you write code for the web.

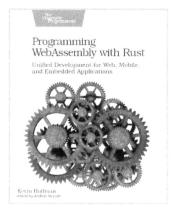

Kevin Hoffman
(238 pages) ISBN: 9781680506365. $45.95
https://pragprog.com/book/khrust

Pandas Brain Teasers

This book contains 25 short programs that will challenge your understanding of Pandas. Like any big project, the Pandas developers had to make some design decisions that at times seem surprising. This book uses those quirks as a teaching opportunity. By understanding the gaps in your knowledge, you'll become better at what you do. Some of the teasers are from the author's experience shipping bugs to production, and some from others doing the same. Teasers and puzzles are fun, and learning how to solve them can teach you to avoid programming mistakes and maybe even impress your colleagues and future employers.

Miki Tebeka

(110 pages) ISBN: 9781680509014. $18.95

https://pragprog.com/book/d-pandas

Go Brain Teasers

This book contains 25 short programs that will challenge your understanding of Go. Like any big project, the Go developers had to make some design decisions that at times seem surprising. This book uses those quirks as a teaching opportunity. By understanding the gaps in your knowledge, you'll become better at what you do. Some of the teasers are from the author's experience shipping bugs to production, and some from others doing the same. Teasers and puzzles are fun, and learning how to solve them can teach you to avoid programming mistakes and maybe even impress your colleagues and future employers.

Miki Tebeka

(110 pages) ISBN: 9781680508994. $18.95

https://pragprog.com/book/d-gobrain

Python Brain Teasers

We geeks love puzzles and solving them. The Python programming language is a simple one, but like all other languages it has quirks. This book uses those quirks as teaching opportunities via 30 simple Python programs that challenge your understanding of Python. The teasers will help you avoid mistakes, see gaps in your knowledge, and become better at what you do. Use these teasers to impress your co-workers or just to pass the time in those boring meetings. Teasers are fun!

Miki Tebeka
(116 pages) ISBN: 9781680509007. $18.95
https://pragprog.com/book/d-pybrain

Practical Programming, Third Edition

Classroom-tested by tens of thousands of students, this new edition of the best-selling intro to programming book is for anyone who wants to understand computer science. Learn about design, algorithms, testing, and debugging. Discover the fundamentals of programming with Python 3.6—a language that's used in millions of devices. Write programs to solve real-world problems, and come away with everything you need to produce quality code. This edition has been updated to use the new language features in Python 3.6.

Paul Gries, Jennifer Campbell, Jason Montojo
(410 pages) ISBN: 9781680502688. $49.95
https://pragprog.com/book/gwpy3

Kotlin and Android Development featuring Jetpack

Start building native Android apps the modern way in Kotlin with Jetpack's expansive set of tools, libraries, and best practices. Learn how to create efficient, resilient views with Fragments and share data between the views with ViewModels. Use Room to persist valuable data quickly, and avoid NullPointerExceptions and Java's verbose expressions with Kotlin. You can even handle asynchronous web service calls elegantly with Kotlin coroutines. Achieve all of this and much more while building two full-featured apps, following detailed, step-by-step instructions.

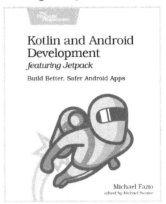

Michael Fazio
(444 pages) ISBN: 9781680508154. $49.95
https://pragprog.com/book/mfjetpack

Modern CSS with Tailwind

Tailwind CSS is an exciting new CSS framework that allows you to design your site by composing simple utility classes to create complex effects. With Tailwind, you can style your text, move your items on the page, design complex page layouts, and adapt your design for devices from a phone to a wide-screen monitor. With this book, you'll learn how to use the Tailwind for its flexibility and its consistency, from the smallest detail of your typography to the entire design of your site.

Noel Rappin
(90 pages) ISBN: 9781680508185. $26.95
https://pragprog.com/book/tailwind

The Pragmatic Bookshelf

The Pragmatic Bookshelf features books written by professional developers for professional developers. The titles continue the well-known Pragmatic Programmer style and continue to garner awards and rave reviews. As development gets more and more difficult, the Pragmatic Programmers will be there with more titles and products to help you stay on top of your game.

Visit Us Online

This Book's Home Page
https://pragprog.com/book/hwrustbrain
Source code from this book, errata, and other resources. Come give us feedback, too!

Keep Up to Date
https://pragprog.com
Join our announcement mailing list (low volume) or follow us on twitter @pragprog for new titles, sales, coupons, hot tips, and more.

New and Noteworthy
https://pragprog.com/news
Check out the latest pragmatic developments, new titles and other offerings.

Save on the ebook

Save on the ebook versions of this title. Owning the paper version of this book entitles you to purchase the electronic versions at a terrific discount.

PDFs are great for carrying around on your laptop—they are hyperlinked, have color, and are fully searchable. Most titles are also available for the iPhone and iPod touch, Amazon Kindle, and other popular e-book readers.

Send a copy of your receipt to support@pragprog.com and we'll provide you with a discount coupon.

Contact Us

Online Orders:	*https://pragprog.com/catalog*
Customer Service:	*support@pragprog.com*
International Rights:	*translations@pragprog.com*
Academic Use:	*academic@pragprog.com*
Write for Us:	*http://write-for-us.pragprog.com*
Or Call:	+1 800-699-7764

Lightning Source UK Ltd.
Milton Keynes UK
UKHW031823080522
402615UK00004B/11